Legend of Artemis

Artemis, namesake of this journal and goddess of light, had the divine duty of illuminating the darkness. Often she is depicted carrying a candle or torch, lighting the way for others and leading them through territories yet uncharted. Known as the chaste Greek goddess associated with the moon and hunt, her connection with the natural world symbolized her own untamed spirit, and she became the patron saint of childbirth, protector of wild animals, virgins and the powerless. Her illumination lends inspiration to the theme of this edition, *courage of our convictions*, shedding light into the unknown and supporting us with her courage and strength.

Artemis in Paris, *Jeri Rogers*

Artemis

Artemis encourages the development of local art and literature by supporting talent in the Blue Ridge Mountains and beyond.

The theme of *Artemis* 2015 is *Courage of our convictions*. Contributors submitted work reflecting this theme.

The design and layout of *Artemis* is based on Sacred Geometry proportions of Phi, or 1.618. This number is considered to be the fundamental building block of nature. Recurring throughout art, architecture, botany, astronomy, biology and music, this number was named by the Greeks as the "Golden Mean" and also referred to as the Divine Proportion. The primary font used in *Artemis* is from the Berkely family, a modernized version of a classic Goudy old-style font, originally designed for the University of California Press at Berkley in the late 1930's. Rotis San Serif is also used as an accent font.

Guest Artist **Bill White**:
>   Cover Image: *The Taubman Panorama: Taubman View #4 — H&C Coffee, 2011*
>   *Collection of the Taubman Museum of Art; Gift of Bill White, 2015.003.004*

Guest Writer **Beth Macy**:
>   Featured literary piece: *Mining Life Along the Riverbank*

Art Editor: **Jeri Nolan Rogers**
Design Editor: **Virginia Lepley**
Poetry Editor: **Maurice Ferguson**

ISSN # 2374-4057

Printed in the United States of America

Artemis/Artists and Writers, Inc., P.O. Box 505, Floyd, VA 24091. www.ArtemisJournal.org

Photo by David Hungate

Artemis 2015 is dedicated to our guest writer, **Beth Macy**, for her courage of conviction in bringing this story of people and principles to life and to all the factory workers her book, ***Factory Man,*** gave a face and a voice to.

Start right now
take a small step
you can call your own
don't follow
someone else's
heroics, be humble
and focused,
start close in,
don't mistake
*   that other for your own*

~ David Whyte

Table of Contents

Table of Contents

Roaring Run Creek, *Bill White*

Mining Life Along the River Bank

One of the guiding tenets of my journalism comes from the historian Will Durant:

Civilization is a stream with banks. The stream is sometimes filled with blood from people killing, stealing, shouting and doing the things historians usually record; while on the banks, unnoticed, people build homes, make love, raise children, sing songs, write poetry and even whittle statues. The story of civilization is the story of what happened on the banks.

In Henry County, Virginia, an hour south of my home in Roanoke, I found the inspiration for my first book along the banks of the icy, meandering Smith River. It was a hidden gem tucked away amid piles of demolished smokestack bricks. I found pieces of the story in hillside trailer homes and beside nursing-home beds. I felt it in the ghosts of wood shavings and smoke tendrils that had long vanished from the scene.

As a longtime reporter for The Roanoke Times, I had watched my colleagues on our dwindling business team cover factory closings in that region. Then, in 2011, a freelance photographer and friend of mine named Jared Soares took it upon himself to document what the aftermath of those closings looked like, and asked me to collaborate. In the Henry County seat of Martinsville — once Virginia's manufacturing powerhouse, once home to the most millionaires per capita in the country — twenty-thousand jobs had gone away in two decades, first in textiles and then furniture. Factory owners and CEOs had shut the factories down in favor of importing cheaper goods from China, Vietnam, and Indonesia, where workers were paid a fraction of the American workers' rates.

Then, the CEOs put their blinders on. And so did the American consumer. For who among us didn't enjoy the cheaper bath towels and bedroom suites? We all looked the other way while half the workers in the region joined the ranks of the unemployed.

What happens to a community when half its jobs go away? Hadn't anyone at all fought back to keep their factories churning? How did the CEOs sleep at night?

• • •

I could tell right away the story was far more complex than the initial newspaper accounts. "Time equals truth," the great Lyndon Johnson biographer Robert Caro has said.

I needed time to figure out how it came to be that the executives' cars still lined the company parking lots—but the factory workers and their cars had vanished just ahead of the smokestacks, which were now reduced to piles of bricks and empty expanses of manicured grass. Most of the seven factories that had lined the Smith River in Bassett, Virginia were now cordoned off by chain-link fences. Two had fallen prey to fire (one of them arson), and both times former factory workers raced to the scene to witness the conflagration. "It was like going to a funeral for everyone you know," one told me.

Whither the long-time unemployed? They were everywhere, they were nowhere, they were home watching reality TV. I found them pushing lawnmowers in other people's yards and standing in line at area food pantries. For the ones lucky enough to land part-time work after their unemployment expired, I found them behind the checkout counter at Walmart, the company that had been the biggest offshoring champion of all.

Then I searched out the press-avoiding CEOs who'd shut the factories down. I wanted to go beyond the press-release gloss to find out why they'd done it and how they pulled it off. I had to ask dicey questions not just about greed and commerce but also about exploitative labor practices going back generations. In a region where most African-Americans trace their roots to tobacco plantation slavery and sharecropping, I wanted to know: How did the company founders treat their help, both in the factories and in their homes? What did it feel like to wear two girdles at once as a guard against being groped? When the CEO kicked his corporate pilot, did he bleed? How did it feel telling hundreds people they would no longer have a job—did you cry?

Along the way, I interviewed myself: Were the stories people telling me true? Were they fair? And in the grand scheme of humanity, does it matter how the powerful treated the generations of workers who'd helped build their wealth? In the end, I decided that, yes, what transpired in the board rooms and bedrooms really did matter—and it was nothing like what had been reported in the newspapers and annual reports.

People have asked how I managed to take a story about old factories and furniture, and actually make it interesting. To begin with, I looked beyond the official reports and the made-up words (like "offshoring"). I eschewed the vague acronyms meant to occlude the pain of international trade (like "WTO" and "TPP"). I had to talk to actual humans. And just when I thought I'd done enough reporting, I realized I was dead wrong. I needed to talk to so many more.

And by that I mean people who probably don't live in my ZIP code or show up on my Facebook profiles and Twitter feeds. Technology may bridge geography and time zones, but it's no substitute for poking around a community you don't already know, asking nosy questions and writing down what you've heard, seen, and felt.

"You have to be there," says the master, Gay Talese. "You have to see the people. Even if you don't think you're getting that much. ... One of the problems of journalism today is how we are narrowing our focus and becoming indoors in terms of internalizing our reporting. The detail is what I think we're missing."

• • •

I'd all but finished my reporting on the hollowed-out factory communities of Martinsville, Bassett and Henry County when a friendly source took me on a seminal tour. I'd already written about the demolished factories, but it wasn't until I actually saw Harry Ferguson on his backhoe, burying the last literal chunks of the last factory in Bassett, that I understood the story viscerally. "If you'd told people in Bassett 10 years ago that I'd be up here today burying this factory, they'd have said you were a complete fool," he said. Then, he handed me a commemorative brick.

I kept reporting. I attended my own makeshift factory funerals. I journeyed by kayak down the Smith River, the reason the factories were built where they were. I trounced through an overgrown, chigger-filled cemetery searching out the overturned graves of slaves-turned-sharecroppers-turned-furniture factory finishers.

I talked to scores of people who'd lost their jobs to globalization and offshoring over the past fifteen years. Most had a palpable, almost desperate desire to tell me what it was like trying to live on $8.50-an-hour part-time jobs with no benefits, of the indignities they'd suffered in food pantry and Virginia Employment Commission lines.

To buoy me when I felt intimidated or scared, I called on longtime mentors — journalist friends, mostly — who helped me shape my arguments and script some of my toughest phone calls. I showed early drafts to economists, business owners and professors and begged them to point out holes in my logic and errors in my math. If something sounded especially outrageous to me, I called as many people as I could to confirm its veracity until finally I could satisfy myself that a painful detail was true, and its inclusion fair.

I have long taken a "ground-up" approach to storytelling. When I'm writing about immigrants, I eat the posole. If I'm writing about veterans with PTSD who won't look me in the eye, I sit on the floor. If I want to know what's really going on in health care, I shadow not a hospital official but a nurse's aide.

Above all, I pride myself on inclusion. For that I thank a tough editor I had early in my twenties. Her last name was Zomparelli — her marathon editing sessions were known as "Zomp Stomps" — and she had this super-annoying habit of sending my features back to me if they didn't accurately reflect the diversity of our city's population. Quite literally, if one-quarter of Roanoke's population was black, then twenty-five percent of my sources had to be too. Every time. It was the greatest training a young reporter could have.

To get strangers to talk to me, I approach them with a spirit of genuine curiosity. More than any phony arm-twisting tactic, I believe nonjudgmental curiosity is the key to building trust. Before I leave I make sure my subjects know I want to get their story right, to the point of returning to talk to them again and making repeated phone calls. (Some of the best stories in *Factory Man* were revealed to me only after four or five visits to an interviewee's house.)

The challenge of writing a book that spans 110 years, as *Factory Man* did, is presenting the collected stories in a way that illuminates a broader swath of American history. In the book I'm writing now, called *Truevine*, two African-American brothers are sold to the circus in the 1910s and relegated to peonage in the freak show while their mother searches for them to the point of risking her life to win their freedom back. It's a story I first started chasing not long after arriving in Roanoke, Virginia, in 1989. The context is sharecropping in the Jim Crow South, American entertainment before Hollywood, radio and TV; and poverty and hardship in a black Roanoke enclave once known as "Peach and Honey."

Just as I did with *Factory Man*, I'm cobbling together a holy mess of photographs, interviews, academic studies, lawsuit filings, and a pile of books in a process that a writer-friend of mine likens to "laying down track." Somewhere between the hundreds of anecdotes and facts, a living, breathing narrative begins to surface.

On days when I'm lucky enough to divine new meaning from the disparate mishmash of collected feelings and facts, I recall the words of the late writer Brenda Ueland. She said that writing felt to her "not like Lord Byron on a mountaintop, but like a child stringing beads in kindergarten — happy, absorbed, and quietly putting one bead on after another."

On bad days, the doubt creeps in and sidles up. "What gives you the right to tell this family's story of race and greed?" it demands to know. And: "Aren't you just one more white person exploiting people for her own personal ends?"

For courage, I imagine two of my favorite poets whispering in my ear as I type. Billy Collins, in his *Walking Across the Atlantic*, advises us to look below the ocean's surface "to imagine what this must look like to the fish below." David Whyte, in his *Start Close In*, encourages us to:

Start right now
take a small step
you can call your own
don't follow
someone else's
heroics, be humble
and focused,
start close in,
don't mistake
    that other for your own.

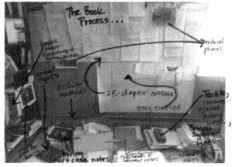

Writing a book is not unlike making a ball out of the rubber bands that arrive on my front porch every morning, stretched around my newspaper. At first the ball is lopsided, its pieces askew — it looks ridiculous. But add enough rubber bands, and something wholly new begins to form. With patience and attention to structure, one day it may even bounce.

• • •

Not long ago, I was asked to speak about *Factory Man* in a private club in Washington, D.C., where I was surrounded by powerful people — high-ranking government officials, past and present; foreign ambassadors, former governors, a few media stars and CEOs of multinational corporations. On a blustery February evening, I was the only woman who'd arrived at the coat check of the posh, storied club not wearing a fur.

A retired executive and former governor took me to task for ridiculing the globalization guru, Tom Friedman, in my book, specifically for my description of his 11,400-square feet mansion.

"It was a cheap shot," the man told me, repeatedly. "I mean, do you have any idea who you're talking to here? The people in this room don't even *know* any factory workers."

Which was exactly my point. The CEO was as out of touch as Friedman, living in his cushy Maryland suburb, in a city that had sailed through the recession with a five percent unemployment rate. These men have not peered beneath the water's surface. They have failed to get on the ground.

They know so little of the displaced people who made sweatshirts and culled lumber that it doesn't move them in the slightest to try to imagine what it's like arriving hours before the food pantries open, some of them leaning on walkers for support — to grab a spot in line.

A few Henry County power brokers have reacted similarly to the book, castigating me for interviewing maids, barbers, babysitters, and discount furniture-store owners. As if the only stories that mattered were their own.

Now more than halfway through the writing of my second book, I keep my commemorative factory brick close. It reminds me to keep showing up and to keep asking questions, even uncomfortable ones. The brick reminds me who my real touchstones are — the people on the riverbanks.

So I cast my net wide. I peer into the water looking for fish.

I interview the cooks, the babysitters, the nurses' aides.

I call the experts. I sleep poorly until the first draft is nailed, fretting about fairness and truth. I read. I call the babysitters back.

Beth Macy

Winter Snow, *Bill White*

The Courage of my Convictions

I knew I wanted to be a painter from about the age of eight and I was fortunate to be supported by my family. I love the feel of oil paint and the touch of the brush to the canvas. Color is magical and capable of expressing so many varied qualities.

When I was in graduate school I had to explain my reasons for painting in a representational way to classmates who were dedicated to such current trends as conceptual art and installations. The constant challenge to my fundamental beliefs was a way to confirm that they are true for me and not just adopted views. I emerged from graduate school feeling that I had confirmed the strength of my convictions and that I am a part of the long tradition of painting. Abstraction and representation are not opposites. To me this is a false dichotomy. My paintings have an underlying abstract structure as well as a depiction of what I see in the world around me. Painting is my means to this end.

Over the decades I have experienced the doubts that arise from competing tendencies; to adopt an idea as the motif or use the immediacy of sensation and feeling. If I "think" while I paint the work grows stiff and lacks the connection with my inner and outer experience. My work is stronger when I am open to discovery through observation while being in the "flow". I seek the unfolding of the work as it happens on the easel right in front of me. Once I knew this about myself it was possible to stay present in the moment of creation.

I believe that from an early age empathy has given me access to deeper human connections that continue to inform my work.

"The poetic quality is not obtained by eschewing any truths of fact or of Nature...Poetry is the vision of reality."
~ George Inness

Bill White
for ***Artemis***, 2015

Nude with Mirror

by Miro

She sits up,
as if the square that rounds her room
has turned her rage
into courage, as if her auto-cylinder
arms and legs revolve,
resolve what troubles her about
her lack of breath. The slow
soft sizzle of her thoughts
fills up every hole and
corner of what she
is not.

When she holds up the mirror
and sees what's inside, she decides
to kill the cat o nine tales
whipping her reflection
to death. The thick braid
that climbs to the top of her head
becomes a little brown
derby. Her right hand turns
into a fist and knuckles the huge drum
she sits on.

What starts to grow there
is the lavish abundance of roses
a butterfly escapes from,
riddling the air with its own
thicket of meaning: "I feel like I've been
reborn," its dizzy flight proclaims,

and the nude's eyelids
close, as if the image it locks up
repeats those words over and over,
so she gets sleepy & slippery
and drops the mirror, claiming
the courage of her convictions as they
fill up the four corners
of the frame with
invisible ink.

Llewellyn McKernan

Untitled, *Linda Atkinson*

Never Giving Up, *Tricia Scott*

At Times Like These

For Maya Angelou

At times like these
We measure our words
Because we are
Measuring a life

A friend was not
Lost nor did she
Transition she
Died

We recognize a good
Life was lead a
Generous heart
Ceases to beat
A hearty laugh will
No longer be
Heard

We measure not
The depth
But the width
Of compassion
And passion
And dreams

We place our love
Gently
On the flowers
    That cover her
Under the clouds
    That embrace her
Into the Earth
    That owns her
And now
    Reclaims her

We will miss her
Spirit Her demands
Her hopes for us
And therefore Herself

At times like these

We are sad

We gather
We comfort
Each other
Yet still
At times like these
We
Properly
Cry

Nikki Giovanni

In Memoriam: Eric Trethewey

An Autumn without you, how can this have happened?
It's your season, Eric, but today your keen glance
Does not follow this gaggle of geese who as always
Soar in their arrow formation due south.

If I did not know better I'd swear they've come
To bear your soul away from the dreaded first bite
Of the frost, from what you called "steel gray November",
The massive unraveling of the leaves.

A cricket has been sliding his bow across
His cello legs for several nights now. My dear friend,
I cannot imagine how many unfinished
Back porch symphonies you still had inside you.

This cold wasp staggers like a punch drunk boxer
And I remember how like Empedocles
You peered into that fiery crater of your own Etna
To conceive "the end of all our resurrections".

The farmers are making their last cuttings of hay.
Only the topmost bloom of our rose-of-Sharon remains
A sort of lofty testament : all things come to an end.
We leaves who remain, wave at half mast for you

You surly, gruff, unrepentant Prometheus fellow
Who gave us your fire, your flame, your passion for years.

Maurice Ferguson

Diamond Cave

For Rick, from Notes of Departure

You come down with me to Diamond Cave, Kentucky,
the end of July. I float my body as shadow on a cave wall
while stalactites hang the world, a garden of horned beasts
dripping.

Ground holds above this hollow. We name each shade
into shape: gargoyle, dwarf, dim fantasy of carrots.
Imagination, old stonecutter, wanders loose.
Then the guide cuts the light.

Mere demonstration beneath sundrench—
the dirt, terra-cotta and hay-dry above. For weeks,
rain has been out of the question. Here the question
is how long does it take to go blind. Hours, days, weeks?

We take lessons from light as we lose it. Now
our eyes empty completely. Bats or demons almost
flutter for my cheek, the guides voice reassuring us
this is nothing.

"…is nothing," he echoes. Nothing, this cold in a deep regio
"See," he announces like a prophet striking a match. Your e
holds mine, a sudden aloneness catching light,
catches fire in the dark.

Katharine Soniat

Elegy ["I think by now the river must be thick"]

For my father

I think by now the river must be thick
    with salmon. Late August, I imagine it

as it was that morning: drizzle needling
    the surface, mist at the banks like a net

settling around us — everything damp
    and shining. That morning, awkward

and heavy in our hip waders, we stalked
    into the current and found our places —

you upstream a few yards and out
    far deeper. You must remember how

the river seeped in over your boots
    and you grew heavier with that defeat.

All day I kept turning to watch you, how
    first you mimed our guide's casting

then cast your invisible line, slicing the sky
    between us; and later, rod in hand, how

you tried — again and again — to find
    that perfect arc, flight of an insect

skimming the river's surface. Perhaps
    you recall I cast my line and reeled in

two small trout we could not keep.
    Because I had to release them, I confess,

I thought about the past — working
    the hooks loose, the fish writhing

in my hands, each one slipping away
    before I could let go. I can tell you now

that I tried to take it all in, record it
    for an elegy I'd write — one day —

when the time came. Your daughter,
    I was that ruthless. What does it matter

if I tell you I learned to be? You kept casting
    your line, and when it did not come back

empty, it was tangled with mine. Some nights,
    dreaming, I step again into the small boat

that carried us out and watch the bank receding —
    my back to where I know we are headed.

Natasha Trethewey

Natasha Trethewey, *"Elegy"* from *Thrall*. Copyright © 2012 by
Natasha Trethewey. Reprinted by permission of Houghton
Mifflin Harcourt. Source: *Thrall* (Houghton Mifflin Harcourt, 2012)

#170 **Falling Fog**, *Caroline Leggett*

November Meditation

In Matthew Arnold's poem, Empedocles in an
evil time has come to a dead end in himself
and speaks of unfixable things, of what
Arnold calls *some root of suffering in himself,/
Some secret and unfollowed vein of woe.*

     *Tonight, at twilight,
the tail-end of autumn, I sit on a hillside
and survey the landscape growing thin*
as an old woman's hair. The maple before me,
half-unleaved, glows pale orange
in the dusk, and the glove-like leaves
of the sweet gum are fingers of flame.
Anguished as the falling leaves appear
in their dry and fiery distortions, something
deep down believes they will come back
again in green. For many years.

But Empedocles on the cone's lip
of Etna no longer believes this,
no longer believes in the possibility
of new leaves fed by the sap of another spring.
Empedocles is beyond us, Beyond me, I suppose,
but not by much, since I'm the one who wants
to hear what it is he wants to say about ends,
deep-ends, the end of all our resurrections.
Though I am not ready to join him
in his terrible logic, I think I believe
at this moment that what he says is true.
The wind that has sprung up, adding
a bite to the air, plucking and tumbling
the dead leaves, seems to believe it too.

Eric Trethewey

Frost on the Fields

so heavy it looks like snow at first.
And ice at the edge of the pond, in the ditches too.
Everything contracts outside and inside.
Sky the cold steel of November,
one more November starving what lives on warmth,
the year gone gaunt with it, the pastures brown,
brown the hillsides and the trees emptied of leaves,
the last of them swept off in a river of wind.

Later, walking, I see the frost has melted.
But the day's hard light does not relent,
reveals all that it touches in keen-edged clarity,
even sodden leaves in the ditches,
a lash of dark birds flicking above the landscape,
bleached grass hugging the earth's skull.
An oak leaf still stemmed to a branch tugs away
and sinks on the wind, the landscape's last lowered flag.
Hunkered on a post, a turkey-buzzard
flaps into ungainly flight as I pass.

Why are we not better than we are?
All around dead leaves lie and then drift
as the day exhales one last breeze, subsides
to a stillness in which the germ of what is not
yet palpable pauses and gathers to begin again.

Eric Trethewey

A Deep River

Brothers and sisters, hum louder, please.
I can feel your vibrations on my neck.
For I aim to speak of a mutual birthright,
the one we created way back when
hanging crimes were not only allowed,

but some folk out there actually used
Noah's curse on Ham as an excuse.

Sorry to say, I was weaned on such.
I knew the weight in my father's hand,
the improvised rumors, the hearsay myths
of separate but equal that kept our kind
cowed and corralled in a harnessed mode.

Religion and business are risky bedfellows.
One won't turn over, the other bellows.

Dear tired and weary, sway in a mystery
of managing harmony while tied to a plow.
Swung low, they were, by a bag of bolls.
Without a Daniel to deliver them.
Those masters believed: to rout rebellion,

train your investment with rites and rotes.
The moans and groans became high notes.

The fields offered up their skinny thighs
and birthed some winged and hopeful rhythms,
some amazing grace and hallelujah
that lit up chambers in a trying place.
Don't think that bones don't rise and cling.

The glory train rings true and long
when its passengers are chained by song.

Our American legacy climbed out of dirt,
and into the finest of orchestra scores.
Today, we're surrounded by all that: jazz.
Jump down, cousins, and turn around.
We do. And yet, we don't cross over.

We stand firm on these stormy fjords;
all bound by the same old haunted chords.

Judy Ayyildiz

Bucolic

Wayward wind gurgles
up-gully & crows branch
high in heroic, peridot,
guardian trees, wings
wrapped & fastened
tight as a soutane,
doom-struck & statuesque,
the miniscule priests
take sanctuary amid
windtorn chaos. Heavy
as a disc-plow & boat-footed,
the melancholic, senescent,
infecund sow lugs
hominy-snout & slop-gut
over dewy, cushioned embankment,
anchoring paunch & trotters
to level, gaping, autumnal
pastureland. Maddened & circling
neurotically, like twilight
charged & speckled with fireflies,
the sheep-dog dives claws-drawn & digs
a low spot down so to skin
spine under lattice,
wiggles to its haunches & moans
into ruddy, blaring, visceral
storm-light. Watching
from an unshuttered, unlatched,
open attic window the atmosphere
unbolt, ecstatic & trembling,
the farmer's daughter,
in her mind, springs rooftop,

New York City Window, *A. Lee Chichester*

her pale, delicate, blue-veined
feet alighting gently on chilled,
electric, tin shingles sizzling
in catastrophic rain & hail,
her mahogany hair wrapped
like a blindfold across her face,
she raises gracefully her arms
into the gail, frail & flimsy
as pipe-cleaners, swooning
euphorically, experiencing
barometric epiphany—equilibrium;
then at last, leaning her slight
weight onto it, she forces it down
with a slate, fierce, proselytic
shriek.

Jason Jones

A Simple Asking

After
hunters and hounds have horned all the land,
foxing, footing, skeltering through moon woods,
after
the woodmen have chopped the farm's fuel,
the smell of acrid chips, the axe and ache, the stack,
store, and stoke of wood,
can you
ink my labors into the calendar of your days
as if the station of my waiting were your destination,
can you
hear this boy's pleasing that secrets
his terrible darkness, drubbing dawn,
the sliver of his cry?

After
jackknives have whistled initials into the tree
as desire's souvenir, seriphed and shadowed,
after
my heroes have carouselled the heavens,
have meteored their verbs
into sparking, blazrng, striking the anvil,
after
wings have hinged their higher blessing,
would you
take my wounds for what they are?

After
the between of *yes* and *no*, the between of
maybe
and *yes*, as wonderful as a gift wrapped idea
after
these dwindling questions, the origami fold
of map, of memory, trust of treaty hands,

will we
know the answer of the heart?
Will we
kiss to our haven the sheer chance, the
after
of our knowing?

Frederick Wilbur

The Ethics of Fallen Apples

"All that is necessary for the triumph of evil is that good men do nothing."
~ attributed to Edmund Burke

Early morning empty street, spilt apples,
a loveliness of fruit turned ugly by their fall.
Frantic, the Trucker scoops them up
to make the half-empty crate seem as it was before.
I witness his gross negligence and his subsequent misdemeanor cover up.
But in his eyes a wordless plea — *I'll be fired*
But we customers of the Garden of Eden Health Food grocery,
we paranoids against a diseased world,
we pilgrims seeking sanctuaries of purity,
we shop here, here on our holy whole-foods site.
But should such violated fruit be offered in our oasis?
But his pleading eyes — *I'll be fired.*
But I must warn everyone.
But he'll be fired. But I must warn everyone. But his pleading eyes.
But, but, my mind is a labyrinth of buts.
Finally the manager appears, inspects the boxes, signs the receipt,
and so bad mercy is triumphant over good ethics
The Trucker thanks me through his moving but silent lips.
But really, spilt apples are just spilt apples and nothing more.
Nevertheless, I presume to give my paranoid fellow pilgrims
the bliss of ignorance;
after all, to this day Eve's nibble on the first fallen apple
blesses and curses us with great wisdom and deep disquiet.

Richard Fein

Rural Village Outside Jinan, China During Spring Festival, *Virginia Lepley*

Sweep Thirteen

In the beginning was a mess,
then the broom
and, not needing a dust pan,
it opened the door.

Buddhist monks sweep the dirt yard,
a leaf falls behind them —
a door to emptiness.

The broom has never
made friends
with permanence.

The orchestra abhors the swish, swish,
but the broom sings its own tune
under the pregnant moon.

Broom erases the snow-covered hill,
the bare ground is a smudge, an insult
until another dusting paints it over.

Wind mimics the broom,
bullies all species of cloud
to exit to
cry somewhere else.

The broom is not a symbol for death,
not a scythe,
but with straight handle,
on occasion, stirs the stars.

Under the rug the broom hides
her children,
stolen words,
spurious conceits.

Frederick Wilbur

Raphine

It is snowing in Raphine.
The path we did not take
is covered with snow,
and now we have parted.
Here I am watching the birds
as they scratch at seed
and thinking of Raphine
and what it means to sew, to sow,
to reap, to grow—and what it means
to take one path instead of another.
And although we were never there,
not on that particular path,
I can see us falling there, like snowflakes,
like snow angels, like two people
who trust each other enough
to fan their arms back and forth
in a frigid Virginia sort of cold—
birds and snow angels and children—
until everything that came before

down that same path we did not take
except in our imagination
is blurred like the history of Raphine,
a little town where men grew things
and women sewed things
and people made machines
that changed the world, then disappeared
the way snow disappears, or fear,
with the sun rising on a new day, or era,
even if it falls so hard and cold
you think it will never thaw,
not in Raphine or Silver Spring
or anywhere we know on earth.
But it doesn't matter because we are warm
inside each other's imagination,
me watching the birds scratch here
and you pouring a cup of coffee there.

Felicia Mitchell

Passage, *Doreen Starling*

Honeycomb

Cigarette burns on windowsills.
Calcified bodies of bees.
Children's fingerprints on glass panes,
names smeared across autumn-steamed windows,
Ann Jane Mary-Kay Gretchen,
signatures as varied as our hair,
brown blonde curly straight short long.

Corncobs in the bedroom walls
where fat rats stashed food for winter.
After the cane fields burned and
the temperatures dropped
they scratched and nibbled
all through the night—
an inch of wall between us,
so close they could hear us breathe.

We snuggled under thin blankets,
listening on windy nights:
pecans pelted the sides of the house,
thuds and plunks on the roof,
gas heaters hissed and purred.
The bones of our old house
creaked and groaned
as we settled in for winter.

Every spring the bees returned,
hotly humming inside the dining room wall.
After school, a sprinkling of thumb-sized bodies
littered the floor where some squeezed in.
Barefoot and hungry
I hopscotched my way to the kitchen
conjuring biscuits and honey.

I imagine honeycombs inside those walls today,
dark gold and time thickened,
hard as amber these decades later.
Are our long-ago words trapped inside, too?
Can voices stick to honey?
Mother reading "The Listeners": *Is anybody there?*
asked the Traveler, knocking on the moonlit door…"

Seasons came and went on the River Road.
And one season, we did not return.

Did we leave part of our selves?
Where do words go?
And the harmony or dissonance
with which they are spoken?
Somewhere inside those walls
surely the hum and tick of our lives
reverberates still
beside quiet honeycomb, decayed corncob.

Are we still there? I wonder,
Traveler and Listener both,
as moonlight shines on the closed door
of our old River Road house.

Jane Goette

Return

After the cutting and the poisons
I take my old dog, who is blind,
Onto the path winding beside the choke cherry and brambles,
The milkweed that bobble their soft, purple flower heads in a small breeze.
We pass beside the creek
Where the black willow stretches out her limbs along the bank
And tosses her hair into the water eddies,
The marsh, where frogs slush into the water at our footsteps,
And the red winged blackbird poses on a high stalk
To fan its brilliant stripe for us.

We step out onto the field that flows away in waves of grasses
To be held by a ring of blue mountains.
The field, where we have watched and smelled and heard and touched
All the seasons dance and turn
And turn again.
We climb the first small rise
And among the sentinels of the orange broom sage,
We lie down.
And my old dog places his muzzle in my palm.

The sky and the clouds of the day pass over us
And the shadows of the trees at the field's edge move across us.
Still we lie there.
The evening swallows stitch the air above us
And the smell of dark gathers.
Still we lie there.
We lie in the field until something ineffable
Passes from the skin of the earth into my skin
And then we rise,
And without stumbling,
Find our way home.

Diane Goff

Missing the TV Killed by a Shotgun

I need
Big scoops of unplugged quiet

I hunger for silent consonants
My favorite mute
Is the *T* in *Tsunami*

I can survive
Weeks and stay moderately sane
Without one image or squeak
Explaining an explosion north of Somewhere

I do miss
That anorexic woman
Who always knew the skinny about everything
I enjoyed her shadow
Each word of hers a Braille scream

John McKernan

Aliens, all Those Years Ago

We brought them religion:
how could we have been so stupid
when we wanted humans to survive?
Now we return and know it's time

to eradicate all need for prayer,
goddesses and gods our toys
shaped to perfection no living being
can achieve in high-heeled shoes.

Ashamed? Shame a purple wash of woe
across our spines, our tentacles
we never should have allowed the shape
of curving glass full of red and blue

light that reaches to polished rows
of augured stone, of painted tile, of wood.
Dark books full of censorious words,
whole lifetimes buried by *should*.

Katharyn Howd Machan

The last Woolworth's lunch counter 1987

The coffee is terrible,
but that's not the point.
This is how
The passing time
Smells, like
grilled cheese
Desperate
hamsters
Disinfected
asbestos tiles.

I am a tourist
alone here except
The waitress,
who is also
The cook,
quiet and overlooking
The goldfish,
bins of unsold alarm
Clocks
waiting.

It feels like
something spilled out
Here years ago
and the mopping-up
Is taking
too long.

My saucer is chipped
at two o'clock.
Feel the foam rubber

under the cracked
Upholstery sparkly red
ragged edges.

There's pie on the stand,
droopy-crusted
Meringue on uneasy
chocolate custard.
How much regret do you
want with your fries?
The mechanical motorcycle
game no-one wants to play,

What do I know?
Me with the two
Powdered creamers
in foiled
Factory packages
and white,
And white
sugar.

Corrugated handrail
on the escalator
Clacks at intervals
sometimes
The door opens
With a sigh

Like leaving for good.

Dave Wiseman

Triple Goddess, *Lauren Cooper*

Litany for Our Lady of Guadalupe

I want to believe I see the last leaf of the season cradle-rock down.

I want to believe I hear hands unclasp as storm winds turn.

I want to believe I carry a cloak like my breath carries on the winds before me.

I want to believe I am asked to open the cloak as if it were a door inside me.

I want to believe I reach after the cloak as it unfolds and begins spilling roses.

I want to believe I take up as many roses as I can to save them.

I want to believe I feel each rose rip from my hands.

I want to believe I am left with only cloak and breath wide before me.

I want to believe I see the stars and moon and sun where there was only cloak and breath.

I want to believe I see a woman cradled in the color of the season's last leaf.

Jose Angel Araguz

Fragile World

For Tim Sewell

This earth of ours is so big and beautiful
When see from above —
The soft curves and the ribbons of blue
Rivers and tan desert and jagged mountains
Trying to tear at the very sky.
This earth turns so slowly it seems
Unmovable, a solid thing anchored
To its spot. But then in a gasp, I realize
It spins so recklessly around the sun
In some wobbly orbit, almost
Untethered to anything, ready to break
Free from all laws and gravity and love.
I stand here — somewhere on the Western
Slope and look out into the desert of
Colorado, and I get cold shivers just
Wondering how any of us hold on
To our places on the Earth.

Sean Prentiss

Becoming a Tree

When my mind ceased
to be my friend, when it
began to bulge with worry,
my friend said, "Become a tree."

In the field behind my house
I lift my arms. Close my eyes.
My trunk quakes just a little. My limbs
give themselves up to the wind.

I sway.

Fittingly, I am wearing brown pants,
a sweater of orange, red, and yellow swirls.
Autumn. I imagine my white hair
auburn again.

I sway.

I accept my rough cheeks, lined
and wrinkled, my pockmarked hands,
recognize the twisting and turning
my body has endured over the years.

I sway.

The bottoms of my feet tingle.
My toes claw the earth,
burrow deeply
into the soil.

I sway.

B. Chelsea Adams

Alone in the Mist, *Kim Dameron*

The Struggle

Don't worry about me; I'm fine
Secrets will not let anyone know
Behind these beautiful eyes
Behind this beautiful smile
Behind these threads, dressed to kill
Inside a plan to tear everything to shreds
There is a city of pain
To get off the bridge
A toll must be paid
City full of lights
Every night awake
Afraid of the dark
You may peek around my soul
Finding all kept in the dark
Discovering all I don't know
Fear that you may understand
Better than I understand of myself
Time is running out
Waiting on the day I admit
I'm lost
Struggling with acceptance
Don't know which way to go
Don't know what to say
Don't know how to feel
I don't even know who I am anymore
Not sure if I ever did
Never learning to embrace myself
Everyone else seemed so cool
I hate to even feel this way
Shame written on my face
Words my mouth wont speak
Haunt me while awake
Making rivers of my eyes
The tears feel great

Compared to the fact
They can see me
This will only be for a moment
A snail returning to its shell
Pride sure enough to kick in
Wearing a new disguise
Don't worry about me; I'm fine
I can get through this on my own
The cold front of defeat invades
Prayers I don't pray
Struggling to believe the unseen
Faith less than a mustard seed
Pride doesn't mention
We can't hide from God
Pride doesn't mention
What's not said, still can be seen
Waiting to admit…
The struggle of the past
Can't seem to let go
Or be honest with my flaws
Afraid of what they may say
How they may feel
The struggle is real
So consumed and blinded
A fresh start
Courage to embrace the past
Without running away
There is a life of my own, but its still not mine
Same creator, different paths
I cant live another life
They could never live mine

Ashley Rhame

After Hearing Sylvia Plath Read "Tulips"

*"I didn't want any flowers, I only wanted / To lie
with my hands turned up and be utterly empty."*
~ Sylvia Plath, "**Tulips**" from Ariel

This day is loathe to start, it's gray,
a dreary sky, blunt pencil stub.
But start it does, as if by will,
a will that warns of laziness.

The light augments, not broad or bright.
It merely grows, so duty-bound.
We guess at motive of surroundings,
assign a gloss to what we see.

Suppose we move, step into action,
right foot, left foot, gaining distance,
maintain illusion that there's purpose,
try to hide from emptiness.

Could we change our tone of voice,
put such words next to each other,
look from someone else's eyes,
and so transform these lives we live?

No way to know until we start,
push our boat from shore to sea,
trust wave enough to throw our net,
if lucky later, finding harbor.

Elizabeth Bodien

The Dawn Horse

"I used to think I could turn myself into a horse."
~ Leonora Carrington

She shot away and pierced the wilderness
That also ran—the larches clumped along
With ancient, humpbacked boxwoods, staggering,
While all the nesting birds tweedled dismay.
Her nanny, blackened like a half-baked log,
Put out her claws to stop this fit of flight,
Her mother pilfered shrieks from peacock throats,
Her father cursed, set loose fox-hunting hounds.
And so she changed her shape, not to a fox
But to a little horse with jet black hide
Who raced in wind and shuddered at the leaves
That rang like bells to call her in for tea.
A little black horse, little white horse, sun
In the outline of a horse and, last, red
Like ochre blown from lips to cavern walls . . .
And she was all these horses till she reached
The city, where she took a woman's shape
Once more, and trussed an antique rocking horse
Against a plaster wall. She ran to love,
Unleashing all her little foxes—kept
A beast, a wild familiar self to bite
Her ankles if she strayed too far in dreams,
To help her conjure shadow from the air,
To make the magic that her men called *art* . . .
Yet all the time, outside the windowpanes,
The little white horse ran and rocked the trees.

Marly Youmans

The Given Only After

the taken. That sequence.
As when

Sweety died and I cried out *but he can't*
he can't fly, not with dirt on his wings

watching as mother's hands scooped dark earth
that swallowed the shoebox, filling the hole we dug

under the bloom-tipped lilac, hearing
he will, tonight in the dark when we sleep

he'll wake and fly up to angels
                     —and how did my mother know

that night by flashlight to go back out
and open the grave, take the body,

bury the box hushed and empty. How did my mother know—
that of her three, only I would run at sunrise out to the yard to scrape

with a flat stone, hand trembling, and pull off the dirt-damp cardboard lid
to a single blue feather, to a belief from then forward in any wild

vision, word or wonder, in utter impossibility and dim, sweet
possibilities far beyond the eye's gaze. And much later down the ladder

of heavy years, I knew from lifting that lid, I knew
that all loss could be countered, if not by the slimmest

chance of flight to heaven, then by the wide
love and cunning of others.

Sea and Sky, *Margaret Mar*

Vivian Teter

Attic Window

*"If a young girl slept under a new quilt
she'd dream of the boy she was going to marry."*
~The Foxfire Book

My night is seventeen and willowy.
I stitch myself into sleep as the clouds mend.

The roses are developing into a hundred suns;
in the meadow the creek is a washed mirror.

Bits of books ride in on the night air: a lock of Juliet's hair,
the west wind on moors, harpoons splitting a whale's skin.

East—past Laurel Fork—there's Paris, a great pin
pricking the cotton sky, paint sticking to the streets.

Squinting West, I can see China, her walls seaming
fields where women thrash golden grass at noon.

I will milk at dawn, like Heidi, plaits twisting
about my head, dark ropes meeting,

twin snakes curled in an African basket.
The buffalo thumps, a pulse, over low plains.

My mother will knot teaberry to my waist to draw
a husband out of a mountain, and some dust.

And suddenly I see him, resting on a fallen log.
Canadian butterflies weave between his fingers.

His face is a traced underbelly of the coal mine.
Eyes the color of robins' shells jag his face in half.

Clouds gather like cloth behind his head.
I am skipping stones across some far heart.

The harpoon pierces me and I turn, but my hands are empty.
Like babies they remember nothing.

A patch of sun works its way through the leaves,
turning him into a quilt, unblinking attic pattern

draped over my skin, filling my hands like warm milk.
Morning scratches at the front door.

The quilt folds itself into breakfast,
eggs setting like moons at sunrise.

Pauline Pauley

Old Burmese, 2011, *Sam Krisch*

At the Gates of the Wooden Monastery, 2011, *Sam Krisch*

Meander Scars

In flood, the river brerches its banks
to sever its lazy loops, leaving
its old self in fat crescents, commas, oxbows,
in meander scars which never
quite disappear under frogs, cattails and silt.

Drive any winter highway to notice
flat planes diverging, flowing
into random forests, then returning, only
to arc again a few miles on. They are echoes
of eadier passage, a rendering of memory's contours.

Could it be the same with lover's wounds:
each dancing in a magnetic field
between bee-sweet words and beggar's lice,
each laboring in their distrust, their
difficult grace, to color in their life,
each healing without phantom pain?

Frederick Wilbur

Postcard

after Ryan Russell's "Snow-Capped Bales"

slipped into a book in a waiting room.
At first I struggle with smeared whorls
and faint waves of smudged ink, then sink
to wonder at the lack of date and legible place
of origination. But in bold and easy blue
these letters stroke toward me: *"I painted snow
when I wasn't shoveling."* The blizzard slowing,
a span of field blanketed, and snow-capped bales
brushed warm in gold and lavender note a sun
that's just begun anew one long, unbroken journey.

*

So yes, together with you, stranger
and spirit so kin, I too by turn
will now spend my days
painting the snow
when not shoveling it,
painting cloud after cloud
when back aches
from digging hard, heavy earth
and if silence looms too long,
shaping sounds both bright and dark
into song so loud
snow will shatter back to flakes
and fly. Oh we will make
at last the ground flash silver
its sharpest grin
to meet the shovel's
swift cold blade.

Vivian Teter

Culling

For Beth Macy

In the quietude of rotting leaves,
In the bottom of a hollow,
Where a branch sings of late summer rains
And the ferns are full blown for it's August,
I come to walk my mother's woods.

I fear yellow jackets, snakes, the ache
A tick can bring just by walking over your skin —
The black bear's waver
In an understory
Of beech saplings and running cedar.

Tires and gas tanks litter Reed Creek.
I walk in a four-wheeler track
Through woods timbered over too many times to count
But glorious with laurels on the hill top —
The low green glow of Henry County in the distance.

Annie Woodford

Still

condor
spots
deadcalm
the lowdown
carrion body
(not a breath)
wait and see
this poised
pose of death
a fastidious
hunger—
head
neck
naked
as ever
so gutsy
parasites
won't stick
and afterwards
swoosh unwieldy
bird flies high for
snow-melt to splash
each slick fold clean
then positions
stillness
again.

Katherine Soniat

Low Tide

This is the gift, our last night at the ocean, in fall: a full moon, on the night of a lunar eclipse—not a dramatic one, but a prenumbral eclipse that lays a gray-to-black sliver against the lower edge of the moon, a whisper of the earth's shadow we strain our eyes to see from the porch of this old house on the sand. And when the clouds come and then go, I take a chair out over the dunes and sit at the edge of the water, just above where the low night tide pushes the white foam up the shore, and watch the moon on the water. The sky is vast, and no stars shine, just the bright full moon and the clouds that border, surround, move past it, like continents on a map, and the moon floats in the water. The moon fills the night and the sea. The wind has shifted since the miles-distant nor'easter that roiled the surf earlier this week, and the cloud-continents float back over the moon, bit by bit. The dimmed light is the world I saw if I had ever slept in my great-grandmother's house those years ago by the railroad tracks, a half-imagined silver light, a child's sleep wanderings, a dark cast over everything, as if the world had been printed from a black and white transparency, or was a black and white transparency, everything its dream self, dark and not quite forgetting the light.

Cara Ellen Modisett

Ocean Beach, *Gregory Steerman*

Tasia's Wolftrot, *Kathleen Dawe*

Sky Talk

My friend looks at clouds
in the stream, wondering
how close one can be to
another and still be free.
Violets share the forest
floor, cinqfoil, and hepatica,
the names separating a few
that blossom there. Her dog
runs on a boulder, a tail up-
setting flotillas of needle-flies
on the surface. He's heavier
this year and growing older.
The winter she found him,
he was a stray asleep in a
magical doghouse set deep
in the woods, and when fed,
he licked the spoon delicately
as if in training for tea with
a queen. Finally taken home,
and at no loss for what to do,
he claimed each bed and cushion.
                          Some feral dog
of the wild, with a cloud of past-life experiences,
of the domestic sort.
                 Ten years later, he dozes—
an animal that wags a tail and, these days, goes by the name
of Chupi. Folk wisdom says that once you look up and smile,
what's beneath the sky becomes a lot less solid.

Katherine Soniat

Passtime

I mark the patterned weather,
the design of the slow, returning
whale.
             Clouds roll in, each shape
a whole new species with no purpose
yet in mind.

They cast illusion on the rhythm of the whale.

By sundown I want a nocturne of a formal instrument.
Wind blows on the bare branch.
                              It turns me
small,
my shadow long.

Katherine Soniat

Bristow Hardin, Jr. 1920-1975

The period from 1964 to1975 was a tumultuous time in American History. The civil rights movement, voter registration drives in the Deep South, the assassinations of Medgar Evers, John Kennedy, Martin Luther King, Jr, and Bobby Kennedy, black power salutes by American Olympians, and the backlash against change led by white supremacists who struck from positions of government authority or in stealth early morning bombing black churches. It was the birth of Johnson's War on Poverty and the launching of 1,200 community action agencies across this country. It was the beginning of Total Action Against Poverty.

At the helm of this new and unconventional agency committed to justice and local change in the urban and rural jurisdiction of the Roanoke Valley was the unconventional Bristow Hardin, World War II Navy enlisted man, musician, accomplished actor, educator, Episcopalian layman. He was smart, confident, funny, ingratiating, and fully committed to bringing opportunity to those who had been born into poverty. Above all he was a man of courage. He stood his ground when challenged by local reporters, the FBI, the KKK which burned a Head Start bus in the TAP parking lot, and attempts to intimidate him from young black radicals or the police department which followed TAP outreach organizers into local neighborhoods.

In 1968, Bristow was interviewed by a WSLS TV reporter who was tracking down a rumor that an unidentified TAP neighborhood worker was allegedly responsible for a fire bombing incident. Bristow responded that he had fully investigated the allegation and was certain that, unless there was something that had not come to his attention, no staff member was responsible for throwing a fire bomb. No one had made, thrown, or taught someone to make or throw a fire bomb. It was the TAP strategy to suggest only positive legal steps to solving a problem and TAP not only did not condone violence but worked for peace, harmony, love and justice. The reporter then got down to an issue that he thought had legs, saying "We are told that TAP hires felons." Bristow responded, "Of course we do. We are in the business of rehabilitation. We require that they have served their time and are on parole. What would you have us do, shoot them or put them on welfare?"

TAP's Founder, Cabell Brand had arranged for thirty business leaders of the Young Presidents Organization to participate in a week long seminar on poverty. To prepare for this seminar, six senior staff members had assembled around Bristow's desk in his office, planning a program that would include: individual luncheon interviews with a woman on Aid to Families with Dependent Children who would tell the business leader about poverty first hand, participation in a poverty simulation game that I had created, a full-day tour of TAP programs, and a closing discussion.

Suddenly, there was a loud knock on the door to Bristow's office. Bristow had an open door policy, but the rule was that if he did not answer it meant that he was busy and the person wanting his attention should go away and come back at another time. No answer. Knock...knock.... knock ....knock...

"All right you son of a bitch, if you want to come in so badly slip your ass in under the door," Bristow finally said.

The door opened, revealing a clean shaven man with white hair in a business suit and trench coat. When Bristow asked who he was, the visitor answered "I am agent Settles of the FBI and I am not used to being treated in such a fashion."

Bristow, shrugging apologetically but with feet on desk, replied "Well, it happens. What can I do for you?"
"It is imperative that I meet with you on an important matter!"
"Well I am busy now and don't have time to meet today."
"This is a serious matter of national security."
"I guess I can give you ten minutes."

The rest of us were glad to get out of the room. Word was that J.Edgar Hoover was already wire taping Martin Luther King, Jr. Rumors were that there were FBI files on all anti-poverty workers.

After agent Settles had laid out the evidence that TAP was in the business of starting a Black Panther organization with federal funds, Bristow sent the following letter to J. Edgar Hoover of the FBI:

"Dear Mr. Hoover: Agent Settles has accused TAP of starting a Black Panther organization with federal funds. The evidence is an endorsed TAP check for $11.87 for some Black Panther literature. I would like to assure you that if we are involved in such an undertaking this will be the most cost effective Black Panther organization in the country costing only eleven dollars and eighty seven cents. I am hereby recommending Agent Settles for early retirement."

Early on in my career at TAP, Bristow's usual travel companion, Wilma Warren, had declined to go with him to a community action conference on the West Coast. When I volunteered, Bristow explained to me that I could go if I agreed to take some vacation time and pay my own expenses to take a one week trip with him to Mexico.

I had long decided that Bristow was my Ph.D.-equivalent education. I desperately wanted to understand what he knew about people, organizations, the use of power, and dealing with conflict, so I enthusiastically made travel plans. For the next week we traveled throughout Mexico, ending up in Oaxaca, a place that Bristow referred to as "Ox-tale." On the second evening of our stay in Acapulco, I persuaded Bristow to leave the comfort of the air-conditioned hotel. He suggested a bull fight held in the local stadium.

Now, a bull fight, despite Ernest Hemingway's glorification of its savagery in his *Death in the Afternoon*, is a rather depressingly brutish exhibition of man's power over nature. The bull is psychologically stressed by the matador's cape which holds no target. The muscles in his neck are pierced and torn by the picadors' lances, which remain embedded in the bull. The majestic animal is confused by the yelling in the stadium and physically fatigued by exertion and loses focus. The matador then seeks permission to kill the bull and slays it by coming over its head, embedding his sword between the animal's shoulder blades and piercing the bull's heart.

The first three bulls went through the customary ritual and were summarily dispatched. Each time, a rope was lassoed around the horns of the dead animal which was dragged by a horse out of the ring. It was another matter with the fourth bull. On one of the passes, the bull dodged the matador's cape and caught the matador around the leg and rolled him across the stadium. Bristow, twice the size of the average Mexican there, was immediately on his feet, screaming, "Bravo, El Toro! Bravo, El Toro, Ole!" Fans across the stadium stared perplexed at this drama developing in the stands. Having just finished The Ugly American, I tried to dissociate myself from Bristow by turning away.

The matador brushed himself off and resumed his trade. Again, the bull caught him around the leg and rolled him to the other side of the ring. Bristow was on his feet with a tirade of approbation for the bull.

To my astonishment, fans across the stadium began to stand and yell for the bull. Sensing that things were getting out of hand, the matador signaled the judges to be allowed to slay the bull and regain his dignity. Permission was granted, much to the objection of Bristow and his followers who were now imitating Bristow's two handed thumbs down gesture. By now I felt it safe to join and was on my feet. However, when the matador's second sword attempt hit shoulder bone, the sword bent like a toothpick and bounced across the stadium floor. Bristow had the crowd on its feet in a tumult of derision for the matador and praise for the bull. When the humbled matador again asked permission from the judges for another kill attempt, everyone was on their feet screaming at the top of their lungs and displaying the thumbs down gesture. That was the day that Bristow Hardin Jr. saved the bull in Acapulco.

Wilma Warren said that Bristow loved to sing a song whose lyrics spelled out his philosophy of change. "One man can awaken another. The second can arouse his next door brother. The three can rouse a town by turning the whole place upside down. The many awake can make such a fuss that finally awakes the rest of us. One man with dawn in his eyes….multiplies." I saw it happen in Acapulco.

It was from the live theater that many of Bristow's management principles were taken. Heading the list of those admonitions were:

"The Play is the thing!" Nothing was more important than the end product, the reason for being. In the theater it was the performance. At TAP it was our mission to side with the poor in their effort to extricate themselves from poverty. We were there to side with the single mother, the family who had no running water, ex-offender trying to get on his feet, the resident of slum rental housing, the unemployed without job skills.

"No shoddy performances!" Excellence was the only acceptable standard. In the theater it meant perfection each and every night. At TAP it meant going the extra mile to make sure that there was real positive impact on the low-income individuals, families, and communities for which we were responsible.

"No prima donnas!" On the stage it was the responsibility of each actor to do her best and to work in concert with the other actors to put on their best performance. At TAP there was no room for showboating and undercutting another staff person in order to promote oneself. The premium was on teamwork. At the end of a theatrical performance everyone bows together.

"There can only be one director!" At TAP, as in the theater, all suggestions were encouraged. However, when a decision had to be made, the director had to make it. The other members of the team were expected to support that decision. The executive would either spend his or her time struggling for control or establish control and be able to share that power and authority with talented leadership. Bristow did not intend to struggle for control.

Bristow died in the early summer of 1975. The following article was written in The Roanoke Times and World News on June 24th:

Bristow Hardin, who left his imprint on the valley's Total Action Against Poverty with all the heft, personality and passion he could muster appropriately left a huge legacy: the lesson that people come first.

He learned, in the first few months with TAP, that no administrative text-book, no set of managerial principles, no 'helpful hints' would do him much good in his search for a solid program for the valley's poor. So he flew by the seat of his ample, baggy pants: cajoling, blustering, demanding loyalty from those under him and earning begrudging admiration from those who had dealings with TAP of those early days.

But always, people came first: the poor, because they had been on the "outs" so long that they needed far more than money alone; businessmen, because their support gave the program a local impetus that all the federal money couldn't provide; TAP workers, because their devotion alone could turn a potential bureaucratic jumble into a believable instrument.

TAP has always had to both discover and toe that fine line between success with the poor and 'respectability' with the rest of the population; Bristow Hardin may well have been the only one willing to play that kind of game.

Another administrator, perhaps with more raw administrative talent and less dramatic flair and determination, would have quit out of sheer exasperation or exhaustion. A slick, public-relations type might have scored well among the affluent, but would have bombed among blacks.

Anyone less than a person with a mission—and that is what TAP was for Bristow Hardin—would have turned the organization into a perfectly proper efficient, 'model' antipoverty agency…that wouldn't have accomplished a thing.

He was outlandish, bumptious, controversial and idealistic; but he was also pragmatic and ingratiating. If he was the center of TAP, life—throbbing and teeming—was at his center. What TAP will need to replace him is not just a head, but a heart." [1]

Excerpts from *"Executive Leadership," Navigating the Nonprofit Rapids: Strategies and Tactics for Running a Nonprofit Company* to be published by Writelife Publishing, an imprint of Boutique of Quality Books Publishing, April 12, 2016. Ted Edlich succeeded Hardin as TAP CEO until his retirement January 31, 2015.

[1] *Roanoke World News editorial: "Bristow Hardin: Lesson in Living," June 24, 1975.*

Ted Edlich

Navigating the Stars, *Gina Louthian-Stanley*

The Tenth Dress

In Modoc legend, Kumush the great father cannot
bear his daughter's plea for her tenth dress

"But Father, your words wove
this dress first, humming every inch
of its buckskin into a song of white shells.
You taught me its meaning many summers ago.
Why won't you now bring it to me?"

"What is wrong with this dress, the one
for after you bathe? Or this one, the one
for digging roots? How small now the dress
for you at seven! But take this one: the one
for gathering wood." Like Kumush my father

holds tight to the tenth dress. Each week
he brings instead a new t-shirt,
each week he searches store aisles
for a larger pair of slippers
though she will not walk again.

But to be by his youngest daughter's side
Kumush finally sees what he must do:
"When I give you this tenth dress, my child,
I shall travel with you. I shall leave my body
on the earth, but I shall not die."

"Father, are your eyes closed?
Only those with closed eyes who lie down
and become dry bone, only they can see
to follow the path of the setting sun."
And so my father dozes

in my sister's room, facing the window
where the sky flares into fire and fades
Pennsylvania farm fields. Shared breaths
in a small room, see how each night
he leaves the nursing home

and each sunrise he returns
bringing her spirit back. Like Kumush
he makes himself small, so small
my sister slips him into a crack far up
in a corner of the great house below the world.

It is a world of drums and speech,
high voices and sweet music that rings
beyond human ears. And come daylight
she disappears, come dawn she vanishes,
singing a song falling soft on his skin as rain.

And so my father journeys back, waking
in a body he has carried eighty two years.
With arms now empty of dresses,
he groans from some vast deep all loss
of language

then wild-eyed, his palms upward and burning
he rushes toward my arms the heavy blanket
that wrapped her last breath.
My hands taking it
translate from flame

what must be passed forward:
the secret of how to carry with us
all light from those who came before,
with greatest care, and in praise
for as long as we walk this earth.

After C.J. Brafford's *Kumush and His Daughter*, a Modoc
creation story in *Dancing Colors: Paths of Native American Women*

Where is the daylily's ancestor?

What and where is the daylily's ancestor?
At the edge of marshes and woodlands, a clue
is blown across the landscape in a crew
of blue birds and bob whites. One elector
only will there be to sway a nothing
vote. Now that it is summer the northward
flocks are leaving for a sunny orchard.
I saw the birds but they were alarming
like the old woman's pink collapsible cup
for camping and pills. Or upset by the charred
meat itself, they make their emissary
selves in a beeline for better parks, nonstop,
all the way to Canada. The seeds trusted
the fallen earth, left there ostensibly..

Laura Close

Touch-me-nots

It's mid-July and jewelweed banks the road.
In summer, green grows languid in the woods
with orange and yellow blossoms all aglow.

One summer hike you carried the heavy load
when nettles stung our legs and drew your blood
in mid-July when jewelweed banked the road.

I dipped their leaves in water til they shone
then rubbed them on your skin right where we stood
with orange and yellow blossoms all aglow.

Smitten by a natural cure bestowed
you bid me lie with you, then said we should
between the tallest jewelweed and the road.

For many summers a single track we wove
through fern lined thickets spiced with cedarwood
and orange and yellow blossoms all aglow.

But since you're gone I walk this path alone.
Touch-me-nots court memories with their pods
hung on verdant shrubs beside the road
with orange and yellow blossoms all aglow.

Molly O'Dell

Take A Hike, *Ken Stockton*

The Widow

She trails a black shadow,
long as a black train.
Eyes rimmed with black, she stares
outwards and inwards. She has
no sex or dreams.
Those who want her
are stung with a black fire
that flows like wind
from her belly.
Clay earth and black tides
are all she sees.
She must wear
a crushed black veil,
hard black shoes,
sit in the darkest corner of the dance room.

Until one morning she wakes
to the crooked apple tree accepting
the thin rain
and knows it's time to begin again.
She pulls off the black veil,
kicks off the black shoes,
kisses the mirror,
smiles at a darting bird,
runs through wet grass,
wanders as if half-mad, the old byways.

At last, no longer careful, she enters the house
of the dead, throws open
the curtains of numbness,
and lets in, not only sunlight,
but also, pain.

Irene Wellman

Coming Into Grace, *Francis Curtis Barnhart*

On Having Come Through I

After the divorce, the calamity,
all that,
Comes the pause, comes breath, comes fire,

Poised in the scent of dreams
Tuned to the sound
of poplar trees flowering
or the bell-like sound of rain

I prepare for the glint of fresh waters,
For the hint of knowing something new
for first strokes
clear light
an expectation of surprises

I hum to myself
to the world
to the beginning.

Francis Curtis Barnhart

Advice for the Young Poet

If you intend such a path through the woods,
take the less traveled, as Frost did
gazing up at maples suppliant with red-tipped leaves.
Don't come back, sore-eyed, from work
every night heaving groceries,
or spend decades under the thumb
of someone who has no thought for you,
so you secretly write at the end of notebooks,
hide letters and poems in plastic bags pushed
into the back of closets.

Don't, like the cockroaches in lonely cities,
come out only when lights are off,
and with your mind at last clear
of the shock of someone's rage,
or the TV's endless chatter,
write down in moonlight
how a mockingbird called
as you left your car and went up steps,
how the leaves have sunk shapes
in the concrete, like hands.

No, you have the right
to shake your fist at the man
with the murderous saw
who cut down the tree
where the bird sang,
and to run far away
and take with you
the words you've made.

Irene Wellman

The Astrologer's Lament

I worry of not possessing any skills to survive.
    The alchemy of taking what's around,

turning it into food and shelter, knowing something
    of fighting off panic and keeping track

of where I've been eludes me. I know little beyond
    my charts of rising and descendant

selves. When Armageddon comes, run, and run
    from me. I will be too busy

waiting for a night I know will come, a night dark
    and moonless, where sounds will rise on the air

a little louder, and a little more unknown, a night
    when we will look to see what is there

and see only stars, and feel the need to know more
    about ourselves in their light.

Jose Angel Araguz

Standing on Charles Darwin

Through Westminster Abbey where Elizabeth Regina rests
above her cousin, eternally dominant in the line of queens,
we thump along the floor, stopping where our guide begins
to point out Edward the Confessor's bier, then other tombs of stone
where only bones remain that once were the cream of England's people:
kings and queens, poets and philosophers, all in crypts below
or honored by marble busts and plaques along its walls.

I stop against a screen while experts intone the exploits of the dead.
Above the stones within breathing distance of the Poet's Corner
I glance down to gasp at Darwin's name engraved
on the very stone I'm standing on.

A scientist buried within Britain's sacred shrine!
One who cracked the pillars of the Church,
a Victorian renegade, who brought back a mental virus from Galapagos
to infect the faith of Christendom!

Why did the monks inter his bones right here,
the bones of this English naturalist who followed the descent of man
down into the skeleton of apes?
Why did they preserve under these stones
the remains of one who denied
that divine breath exhaled into the first man's lungs
and that his body sprang out of dust molded by a Creator's hand?

Since Darwin's body has rested underneath this Abbey
for more than a hundred years,
would his spirit, if he ever had one, and if it could speak,
recant his theory and the million years
it took for man to rise to the summit of the chain of being
but shout instead that it was the Great Cosmic Mind
that needed only six explosive days to speak into existence all there is?

Or would he still stand as firmly on the evidence he gathered
as I myself am standing on him now that only the fittest still survive,
that natural selection steers the evolutionary wheel,
that the mystery of mutation can be explained by science
and by the observant eye?

I step off Darwin's stone into the weakening sunlight
filtered through apostles, prophets, and the Christ
ensconced within the frames of stained glass windows.
In minutes Holy Communion will begin.
Already choristers in two antiphonal choirs are rehearsing for the Mass,
their voices rising and falling in answer to each other's praise.
Soon a priest extols the merits of the unflappable God,
untouched by the denials of modern man.

The tour is over. I have other sights to see. But as I leave,
my mind rehearses another sort of antiphony:
first, the flapping of the wings of Darwin's pigeons,
his exploration on the Beagle, layers of fossils,
the primeval swamp.

Then, in answer, the chants of the Gregorians,
the hymns of Luther,
the orthodoxy of the Church,
the saving grace of God.

The heavy doors swing open and I step into the street
and into a thousand years of London
that float through the evening fog.
Inside the Abbey, while the lamps are lit,
Charles Darwin's bones remain at rest
under the unyielding floor.

David J. Partie

A Parable for Poppy (1901-1983)

On the old concrete tables at the farmer's market
fronting a box of black cherries,
the tawny local figs, tender-skinned with promise.

As he fills for me the green paper box,
I confess to Tim my first real sin: how through
my grandfather's steep mountain garden,

on our way down to the bus, down and down
past drying cornstalks and the huge,
spraddled tomato plants, down along

arbors of slippin' grapes paper-bagged
against hungry wasps, we children trooped,
our arms filled with new textbooks,

until I slowed to pick the first-ripe figs.
In the glossy late-summer afternoons
my bicycle wheels would crush green acorns,

pale kegs of bitter cheese fit only for squirrels,
but mornings I walked and ate even the tough,
half-ripe figs until one Sunday supper, seated

at the table's laden head, Poppy fumes, "I'm going
to cut those goddamn fig bushes down.
Five years since I planted them, and not one fig."

Mary Boxley Bullington

The Goat Dream, *Eliane Fleck*

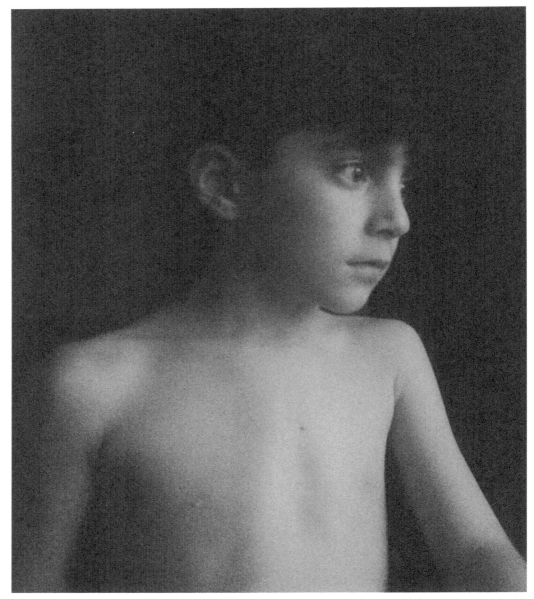

Solitude, *Molly Morikawa Selznick*

The Other Child

In the photograph the Long Island summer home broods over us
like a protective mother. Its cool, dark porches watch us,
a six-year-old boy and a five-year-old girl. We sit side-by-side
on the front steps, in place for the camera.

We both wear white, Randy in a dapper shirt, the collar up,
white shorts, a soft-brimmed hat—the cobalt has already claimed his hair.
I'm in a white pinafore, matching Mary Janes and ankle socks, my hair
held in two high pigtails by white ribbons. Our clothes blaze in the July sunlight.

Randy fiddles with something in the grass beside him.
I study a scratch on my left knee.
We have just had a fight. I am frowning,
but Randy's face remains serene.

I.

He was the son our father needed and had longed for,
the cure our mother had hoped would stop her husband's violence,
the slightly older brother who adored me, named me "Pidge"
because I loved the birds in Central Park,

but then something went stunningly awry
inside my brother's skull.

II.

Near the end, when Randy peed blood into a bag beneath his bed,
no longer walked or stood or ate, when even his last, frail efforts to flirt
with his favorite nurse failed to distract him from the pain chewing up his hours,
I was not allowed to see him.

With my ear pressed against the wall between our rooms,
I heard my brother crying, heard him dying. I yearned
to remind him of those pigeons in the park that waddled,
clucked and bobbed for the peanuts we'd thrown down,

but I was not allowed.

IV.

Right after Randy died,
my father's violence resumed,
and I, the other child, unseen,
sneaked into my brother's room and stole

one tin soldier from his drawer.

Barbara Friedman Stout

This Rope of Intention

Her words—a twisted rope to grab
and fling myself into the eye of fear.
My undone deeds festered, ached;
they sensed her cord of spoken light.
I wrapped myself around a chance to heal,
to softly touch my abuelita's face.

Undone.

What I wanted was to care for her, to feed the one
who told me stories with a hug,
who held my hand while picking *calabazas* from the garden,
who brought *queque* with kindness to her neighbors,
who showed me how to plant a seed
to grow not only trees but also life-long friends,
who trusted me to be her voice when she was losing hers.

I missed Abuelita for eight months.
My uncle said I wasn't welcome:
Would a bullet from a gun greet me at the door?
My crime was that I cleaned her house
while he was cleaning out her bank account,
and so her lying in the hospital also was opportunity.

Come. See me now.
I'm here. Tell everyone good-bye for me.

I swallowed what she said,
felt the echo in my belly like a wave
or undulating knot
that pushed my hands, my feet,
and came undone; her verbal arrow
found its mark. I flew from California to New Mexico
intent to leave when she was safe
or when, unspoken, she—
or I—
was dead.

Karen S. Córdova

Perfumes of Abandonment

He is the traveler's face
treading darkness
and wishing he had the art
to draw love from the wind.

On this strange street
he is the stranger
who dissolves himself
in the gray rain.

He finds the keys
to his unlocked door
in someone else's pocket
and hears his beloved sing.

But it is the open doorway
of the bakery that draws
memories of stories
his grandmother told

as she played
the curls of his head
with hands that kneaded
his dinner.

It is the windborne garden
cutting dreams of roses
to lay love
at the feet of another's wife.

He has been cast out
of such dreams.
He has been reborn
in an alien shape.

And ghosts of his grandmother
and of his beloved
bear truths of aromas
from a rose and a loaf of bread.

David Anthony Sam

Yellow Rose, *Lauren Jonik*

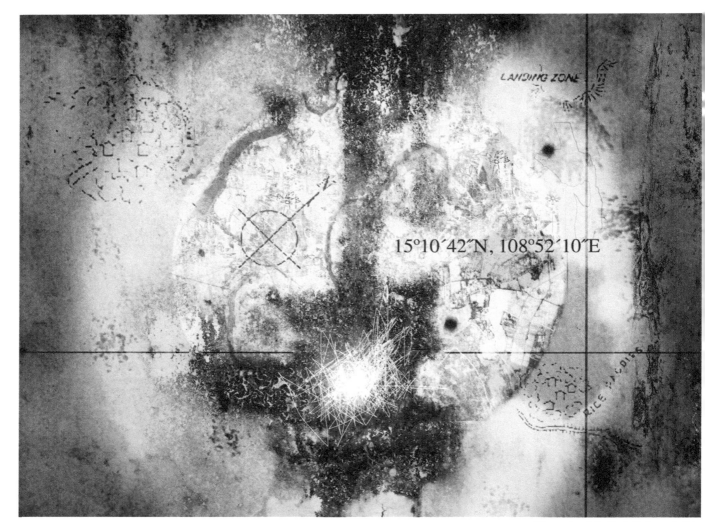

15°10´42″N, 108°52´10″E

Elegy for My Lal, *Robert Sulkin*

Mountain Stranger

Born of African ancestry
You crawled across an ocean
To perform a slow-speed orogenic dance

You spent your youth growing tall and rugged
      cutting a fitting silhouette against a steel-grey sky;
stately and snow-covered — uniquely Appalachian —
You towered over the landscape in your prime

Now in your twilight years
      You slump and sag, wrinkled and furrowed
And call to me with your foreign, mysterious ways

But foreign is also familiar:
Spring brings dogwood and serviceberry, mayapple and ladyslipper —
      a chorus of spring peepers haunts your dark coves;
Summer burns hot on dry ridges of black shale
      splintered by pine and scrub oak;
Fall ushers in an elegaic blend
      of mist-covered hollows and purple blackgum;
Winter washes out color, leaving behind
      grey tree trunks and clear, rushing streams

Black Horse Gap to Tar Hollow Creek
I explore your creases and folds;
Spec Mines Branch to Chair Rock Ridge
I am startled by grouse and black bear

Harvey's Knob hawks glide on rising thermals
As yellow poplar leaves slowly carpet still-warm Earth;
Slick moss grows on shiny wet rocks
Beside creeks darkened with damp rhododendron

You're a stranger worth knowing
You've wisdom worth sharing
I've spent a life in your shadow
Mountain stranger no more

Tim Miller

Tree of Life

Trees in spring get dressed for bright emergence.
In summer they offer us a fan of song and yawning shade.
In autumn those astounding colors belie a simple chemistry of death.
Three seasons of the year we see only their distracting outer show.

How I've longed to strip a summer tree
to see her bare bones out of season,
to reveal that rack of scarred and startled antlers
holding some dark vibrating nest, or hiding a perfect moon.

With every leaf picked clean,
the epic of a long life exposed,
I better understand the significance of rising from a womb of stone
or being robbed of sunlight by a more ambitious neighbor.

Our stories, like the trees', will be abruptly published in the winter of our lives.
It's only on the backs and bristle of ancient giants that glory ever came to us at all.
It's typically in the half forgotten litter of our lives (the decades of faithfully dropped leaves)
that our young begin to decipher the maps for their own deep living.

When silent winter and unmitigated night truly fall upon us
we will approach the old ancestral logs
humbly asking them to burn bright again on our hearths
and in our dreams describe the Tree of Life.

.

Rosemary Wyman

Kafka's Gray

He's tinkering with the knob
to coax a bit of steam into the useless radiator
beside the window—iron-tinted iron.

A cold room, no one to bring him a warm towel,
a cup of tea with the crème he misses
almost more than his mother.

Ever since summer left, taking its greens,
the city seems dirty. A small window faces
the street. The jackdaw's plumage

has changed to *Payne's gray*, claws
ropey against the branch of a Linden tree
near his father's shop. Jackdaw—

kavka in Czech, pronounced *kafka*, emblem
adopted for a shop of fine goods.
He's remembering the red-gray scarf

shivering a little when the door swung open.
Imagining her scent, most popular perfume in Berlin,
as, in his daydreams, the hound's-tooth pattern

caressed her neck. It hung there for weeks,
until a widow came and took it home
for her daughter.

He's speaking to himself in his room
as he writes letters, mouths words,
the High German mixed with Yiddish.

He's thinking back to the time
when he had a woman on his arm.
The clouds carbon on bone.

and nothing to do about winter
than keep the elder Kafka at bay.
Father of fine goods, father of daughters.

Hermann's strength, health and appetite
too large a figure for this street glazed snow
punctuated by ivory lamps.

Judith Skillman

Almost Different

This spring the yellows indicated that I would at last
Remain alive. Forsythia blooms and creasy salad

Tops seemed far from Faulkner's ochre mud.
I would lie flat on towel covered

Grass praising myself as well as all bees and bugs
For miraculously surviving daily

Winter storms. But when the cows began to
Wade out in the pond and stand where the water

Just covered the curve of their bellies
Something draped with an awful surgeon green uneven

On wheels squeaking needing oil rolled me away to
See another June without a complete year behind it.

Here all the shapes in every rock
Resemble the salty pillars of the wife of Lot

And here is my favorite yellow, the porch light
Glow of my childhood home

Janet Fitch-Johnson

Innamorata

She is a prize beauty, and virtuous,
who diligently keeps house, never dances,
not even at Whitsuntide, or on feast days,
who turns hands (as pale as orchids, or bones)

to work, doing no more harm than an old man
with a glass of schnapps. She places her heart
on the doorstep, where it cannot distract her
with fancies. Instead, she clenches her fists

into her apron, practicing for childbirth, for rearing;
she spills not a drop of wine from chalice at church,
munches quietly a good piece of rye bread—
tears in her eyes are as round and lovely as acorns

but these are dropped like sweets before children,
you must not entertain them. By now you must realize

that she cannot possibly exist as she is,
so full of goodness, and that whatever creature

is trapped within is capable of things which are
unspeakably sudden. So watch her, draw a circle

in the earth around her, blast her with counter-spells,
sprinkle her hair with lichen, tie a red yarn

around her wrist, importune whatever rough-hewn
icon guards your entryway, lest she turn into a beast,

and kill—a silver leaf, a mist, and vanish.

Amanda Williams

E/motion, *Susan Saandholland*

Golden Kite, *Gwen Cates*

Karma

Saving the sparrow
whose small self
is wound by wire
may not save the cat
half-eaten by coyote.
It may not save even me
from myself, sorrow coiled
around my heart
like a copperhead.
I love my cat.
I love the coyote
that tried to eat the cat.
But I am sad about the cat,
as sad as a woman crying.
I know it is what it is,
this snake that will strike
or not strike,
on any given day,
no matter what I do.
The coyote already came.
The cat may go.
It is what it is, I repeat,
mantra tenacious as mantis,
my breath paired with sorrow
as good as a set of bellows
fanning embers
in a cold hearth.

Felicia Mitchell

Last Walk

On our last walk,
we paused at a kiwi vine,
dormant that time of year
and yet verdant with desire for spring
and fruit and butterflies.
Its mate,
despite the nursery's promise
of a "hardy mate," was dead,
the male of this species
more fragile
than the female,
its brittle vines already compost
where we'd plant a new vine,
we liked to think,
though thinking wouldn't make it so,
come April.
"This is not symbolic,"
I said to my friend.
He did not laugh, but I did, nervous,
noticing how frail he was
and how his steps shuffled
over the frozen ground,
rootless.

Felicia Mitchell

The Night I Met Your Sister / Jaggin on the Fourth of July

For Jenna and John

don't let go I whispered don't let go and
with wooden wands we woke the sleeping night
I lost my moonstruck eyes within the glow
we watched with wonderment the arch of flight

with wooden wands we woke the sleeping night
we gave new life to starlight long past dead
we watched with wonderment the arch of flight
we let out howls and laughed as fingers bled

but now you're like the starlight long past dead
yes now you're just a photogene of sight
we let out howls and cursed as fingers bled
our eyes went cross trying to see the right

yes now you're just a photogene of sight
a lie alive only within my head
my eyes have crossed trying to see the right
my voice grows hoarse from all the prayers I've pled

a lie alive only within my head
my now half empty queen sized bed grows cold
my voice grows hoarse from all the prayers I've pled
I'm burned because I hold too tight I'm told

as my half empty queen sized bed grows cold
I light the fuse and follow flame along
I'm burned because I hold too tight I'm told
you have to hold on loosely like the song

I light the fuse and follow flame along
I lose my bloodshot eyes within the glow
you have to hold on loosely like the song
but don't let go I counter don't let go.

Sara Krassin

Why I Can't Marry a WASP from Connecticut:
A Revelation Received While Waiting at 125th Street

I fell in love on 125th Street
watching the snow come down

Her lips opened and closed like a clam
Her Chapstick was moist like unwashed underpants
Her emotions were strawberries being crushed in a blender
She could suspend fear in a movie theater
and watch Anthony Hopkins steal people's tongues

I wanted to be featured
in a wedding announcement with her:

"Eleanor Foster Leech
daughter of Harold Jones Foster Leech
was married to Andrea Jones Chaucer
Daughter of Ant Farm Recipient
Chaucer Foster Jones"

She was reading a book about Namibian psychotics
by her father who taught histrionics at Yale

I was skimming *The New York Post*:
"Bob Dylan dyes his underarm hair blue and white
to support leftist Zionists"

While drug addicts sold tokens on 125th Street,
I felt like a leech of good lineage—
a New Jersey-blooded bacterial organism
who watched *All in the Family*
and attended EST seminars in Piscataway
and smoked at truck stations
where Allen Ginsberg used to urinate

for I had graduated Ocean County College
and could never marry a WASP from Connecticut
or an inebriated socialist from Westchester
or perform bestiality on Maine-bred lobsters
or live off American Home Foods stocks
while reading Wallace Stevens
or date Jewish dermatologists
with epidermal layers of Ivy League inferiority

Eleanor Levine

When I Finally Halt

When I finally halt,
Close my daily whirls,
And bend one last of ear
Over my driving age,
I'll take my halt with her in Virginia,
Suffer weird winters alongside the cardinals,
And edge out together when our feet allows.

Then we'll take our gnarled thumbs to town—
Should there be some change—
To devour fried eggs and grits
In bright diners with seats
A lovely plastic emerald green
And tables decked with delightfully yellow laminated mats,
That boast of glorious Patty Melts
Dripping with cheddar and onions
And waffles with chicken
On those Wednesday Culture Nights.

And there the crowd says: Buzz! Buzz! Buzz!
Boiling over elevated television clatter
Heard the night and each night before.
And the crowd says: Buzz! Buzz! Buzz!
All the more:
Since boys my age cannot hear words but only Buzz!

She says pack up the Flaxseed
And we'll be ready to roll
But I must be leery of this Flaxseed collection
I've a hole in my pockets—one on the right the other on the left.

Once in the faked light,
She says her nerves are strangled and worn
In corrupted directions for a woman of her age

I say my bowels are strangled and worn
From decades of its own raucous comedy

And the crowd says: Buzz! Buzz! Buzz!
And my bowels say: Buzz! Buzz! Buzz!

She says: "I've bunched calves
And I only slept three hours last night."

I loudly consider that this must be my fault
And say: "I've lovely feet for an old fart"

And the crowd says: Buzz! Buzz! Buzz!

Outside, she considers twilight sights from
McAfee's Knob
The cardinals in the woods before
Its wink to Tinker Cliffs and nosey-shaped slat

Outside, I consider her forehead to chin
The exquisite face she maintains
Without so much a touch

Outside, I consider her forehead to chin
Shining despite the eclectic fool beside her

Lord, this is the epic I shall take

Les Epstein

518 Elizabeth Street

She won't give up, the Queen of Parrots,
even though butterflies flood her breath,
even though a cage of filigree
has only one door open. She wears

turquoise shirts stained with golden leaves
and no pearl rings upon her fingers
that offer mango to Baby Blue
and Ara Ara and the small unnamed

Gray African, the wisest. She knows they
will live beyond her when her silver braid
hangs loose, her shoulder's ghost no longer holds
weight of rainbow feathers and sharp dark claws—

but still she fills her Key West mornings
with deep sweet coffee and cinnamon rolls,
macadamia nuts for every bright bird
to grasp, to crack, to swallow.

Katharyn Howd Machan

Bridge

Once you decide to leave,
Then go ahead and go;
Do not delay to grieve
The change in status quo.

Step fast from road to wood
Suspended in the air;
Just trust the likelihood
That here will lead to there.

When you approach the place
Where wood meets road again,
Step on, then stop to face
The span where you have been,

And light it, let it burn,
Prohibit a return.

Jane Blanchard

A Ghazal for JoAnn Asbury

You've hidden bits of yourself in all of this.
What the cold does in dogwood winter, you're doing
now, inside the cloud of witnesses around us.

I remember clearly the advisor warning me
against taking your class that year. But I said yes,
because part of me knew there had to be an us.

I'd heard the word Appalachia all of my life,
but you turned it on in me, put books in my hand,
and grounded me inside this galvanizing us.

Were you greeted by a Massachusetts housewife
or a trucker hatted farmer in Beulah,
who saw God in the witchcraft and earthcraft in us?

Considering your love of ghosts and ancestors
and outcasts who went misunderstood in the night,
I keep waiting for your whispered voice to greet us.

You told me, once, that if they knew what you believed,
they might throw you out of even your left-wing church.
I saw, in you, how the Gospel holds all of us.

I'll bring up the story of Shams again. Your life
in us in his mythology. Whatever work
we do now bears your name. Your light puts light in us.

Matt Prater

Adrienne Rich

the voice of a woman speaking to women
poems   stories   whispers of life

tongue like a knife made of liquid light
moving though sand to fire new crystals

lips open and pushing out air
no matter the walls or tightly closed doors

a woman saying what women must hear
against heavy silence   against our long fear

Katharyn Howd Machan

Velocity Girl, *Eric Francis*

Daybreak in the Blue Ridge, *Michele S.*

The Empty Chair

A suicide, says my principal, *do your
thing*. He retreats, a sigh of relief,
leaving me in charge. Of course.

The Suicide Lady in full swing:
call out the crisis team, print
handouts of helpful hints, plan
for this awful day, including
The Empty Chair.

High school—a full seven periods,
he had no study hall. I run off his
schedule, circle classes in red,
draw my route from room to room,
general in battle mode. Look at his
teacher list, mark who'll fall apart,
send a note, *I'll be there.*

The bell sounds, I straighten my back,
walk to English AP, see the empty chair
where he would be, there in the second
row, grinning, cracking a joke. But just
yesterday he disappeared on the Blue

Ridge Parkway. Said goodbye to friends,
drove away in an old Corvair, put a bullet
through his head, leaving us
with the empty chair.

Can't do it, the teacher says
as she retreats, leaving me with
twenty-three, an hour, an eternity.

Okay, I say, *no Hamlet today. Let's
talk about the empty chair where
Adam would be. Not pretend he's
alive, pretend it's alright, pretend
he's coming back. Don't know
about you, but I'm mad as hell.*

Some burst into tears, flee to see
my colleagues, some check out,
go home for the day, but those
who stay talk and talk and talk.

Esther Whitman Johnson

House Sitting

Where he lives is not a house
It's a garage built of cinder blocks.
Electricity, but no running water.
Darrell bathes in the river, even in winter.
But it's his home and the January flood
Took Darrel's house in its mouth like
A lollipop, sucked it in and slipped it out.
All that night, while the water came and went,
Darrell sat just up the hill wrapped in blankets
Watching over his place the way a parent sits up
With a fevered child. It's maudlin to mention that
It's doubtful anyone ever sat up with Darrell, sick or not,
But some things just shouldn't be edited out, they
Need to left on like a string tied around a finger
Because forgetting is so easy and very little
Is easy for Darrell who has lived here for
As long as anyone can remember,
Who lost everything in the
January flood. Even if his
Everything couldn't
Fill the back of
A pick-up truck

Ann Goethe

Teakettle

1.
How you
persist in any
loneliness;
how you remain,
even in this late day
of the century,
anticipatory.
You, the burnished
ritual of our slaking.
Stalwart, domesticated.
A prophecy of the willed,
sustained, exhalation.
And later, found
in an abandoned home
of the war zone,
a bit of rust, a skein
of dust rising from you
like a soul only might,
into the light.

Produce

The prayer bruise bulges purple
in the middle of his forehead
squat   ham-fisted   burley Cyclops
the greengrocer accosts us
as my sister and I handle
his melons   his oranges   his bananas
no touch   he bellows
we jerk back our hands
scorched by his ire
saliva spews in his diatribe
against American women   *these whores*
these tawdry cunts   befouling the customs of his country.

Behind a dirty curtain at the back of his stall
a wrapped woman tends a lit brazier
two small boys encircling her ankles
flies crawling her headscarf
as we back away   her face follows us
hatred and fear cook
in the cauldron of her eyes.

Diane Porter Goff

eakettle, teakettle,
1 the rubble of this century,
ell us the story
f persistence.
ou say, *thirst*
lways thirst, and *firstly*.
Ve are dry-mouthed,
1nredeemed. Gather
 breath, a steam.
ring that train sound
hat might just be
he sound at the center
f our awful being. Bring
he flood. And we will wait,
up in hand, to receive.

Melanie Almeder

Seven Methods of Invocation

First.
Sunrise over the Blue Ridge: sky a silver redux in layers
of veils, inverted scales of a fish, color of thumbed nickel.
I pray that I will learn to pray.

Second.
There's the story of an Appalachian preacher
kneeling at a rock in the woods of Kentucky.
He spoke to Jesus under trees, each person on the list
represented by a small stone. Sorted, re-sorted, gone over.
The stones stayed even after he'd died.

Third.
Breathing is easier, wordless breaths, lighter
than language. God has more than a stethoscope,
a blind try at hearing the whoosh within a chest.

Fourth.
My sister bought a black rosary,
although she's not Catholic. She needed Hail Marys,
feeling prayer under fingertips.
She carries it in her pocket, like Kleenex or chapstick.
Because you can always use it.

Fifth.
Group prayer on a rainy Sunday morning, late January—
the words rise off the page, prewritten,
gathering, spiraling into ascension.

Sixth.
A meal blessing: grace of a quick nod,
to say thanks. Thanks for—

Seventh.
One heart, hard-shell shellacked, with no crack
A woman prays over it. Asks most especially
for a chisel.

Conclusion.
Form is irrelevant. God answers, but sometime
the answer is no, says the pastor with the kind e
And from the earth voices rise, alleluia, amen.

Pauline Pauley

Winter Song

For Laurelsong Cook Staengl

The woodstove howls like a banshee
for the copperhead I killed in the fall
when it crawled from my dream into the kitchen
and laid at the threshold of girl becoming crone

The washing machine hums like a bard
spins the tale of a black bear intruder
the one that left paw prints in the garden
fresh scat at my front porch door

Thoughts turn to poisoned confrontations
and boundaries that were crossed
I save seeds for Persephone and grieve for Pandora
whose box is unlocked but too heavy to carry home

From an icy window pane
I watch the moon's unrocked cradle
No lullaby for the child left alone

I sleep on the floor by a dying friend's bed
and mark my territory with handwritten poems
The floorboards creak to the tick of time
and the shuffling sound of her breathing

Still, the sun rose radiant in the morning
and I named it after her
I joined friends in a circle at nightfall
held hands while she let go

To a slow low beat of drum
we walked a labyrinth of pine boughs
made bright with lit candles
on the longest night of the year

Under a graveyard of stars
we sang into silence
a community remembrance
of future thresholds to cross.

Colleen Redman

**Tors Distunxit Amicitiamanet (Love Survives
with Death Divides)**, *Page Turner*

Fashion Landscape, *Harkrader*

Rewind The Cowboy

Even if you find nothing in the pocket you just discovered, at least you discovered a pocket.

Are you in love with reason?
Don't fall in love with the man who isn't, or else you'll end up ruined.

Who doesn't secretly love relating to 80s teen movies?
Even when I wasn't in heart-suck/love-struck mourning, I divulged deeply in these flicks like one is
supposed to with a Dostoyevsky novel.

Let him quit you before it is too late for the both of you —
You'll be dripping tears at indiscriminate hours, but it's impossible to say it would be worse.

It is a fate of our time to value shallow absurdity over anything else.
Still every generation hosts the same people (so really it is our fate).

Like 'Heathers', for instance.
I know so many internet personas who cherish the pseudo-slasher flick, just as, before them, another.

Our hearts cheer the rotten scoundrel.
Again it does not move forward.

I spend days sitting in my little pampered chair dreaming of Christian Slater to come back from blowing up.
Who else?

Maybe one of those forlorn cowboys in a late 60s western, who are destined to always walk away.
I am a picker, I can never walk away.

It's easy to love being let down, but I do it anyway.
When reality is too kind I have my delicious 2 1/2 hour reveries, where I can extend them if I wish by using
devilry's hand and hitting rewind.

I am sad, but what poet isn't?
If she says she isn't, she is either a liar or a fool, because deep down there is something haunting her to write.

If she's a fool perhaps she hasn't bore witness to the heartbreak endured by *Ariadne of Crete*, or by
Brooke Shields in *Endless Love*.
Both waiting tirelessly for their psychotically confused lovers.

J.R. Schwartz

Green Shutters

I painted the door green today. The brush, dripping hemlock,
pine—quickening unlike the old tree below, injured in August's harsh lightning.
The way we paint bungalows, a fresh coat over tears and rents.
I live far now from where we wrestled under cottons in shuttered light.
Wishing wings, I ran away to the ridge where they fly
(the kestrel, Cooper's, mocker)
they run
(the buck with autumn antlers)
they skulk, prettily
(the grey fox)
they bark at jets, buzzards and butterflies
(Great White, a dog who remembers nothing). On this hill, green goes *hush*.

But the green of the door brings back my lover he left quickly
after juleps near the river.
Brings back my grandmother tying a ribbon on the braid of a redheaded scamp in cool porch-light
we ran to the creek, caught bream for breakfast.
Shimmery, sun-burn't.
Brings back the verdant shade of Gran's front yard, where we dreaded the war, defied it, and said good-bye
he didn't return.

In Biloxi, the summer storm took green doors, shattered green shutters,
flattened Point Cadet where men fled from old wars. They built boats with oak beams like wide arms
on the Point where people talked in brogue of far seas
and new ones spoke Vietnamese.
They all sailed before dawn and came home after dark,
on Sundays little ones jumping into tap-warm water, squealing. As dolphins do.

Wracked: shotgun houses one and another,
newly painted the spring before in greens, pinks and blues—but mostly whitewash.
In memory: shrimp steam wafting before lunch, pusharatas and spring rolls. In memory.
Old windows reflecting oleanders.
Old men mending nets.

Then, gone.
The men, the windows, the oleanders, the squeals.
The green shutters.

Marjie Gowdy

The New ▮ *Handbook*

a man ▮ ▮
shall have troubles.

If a man lives ▮
he shall die ▮

If a man ▮ ▮
▮ ▮

▮ ▮

conceives ▮
he shall ▮

wear a crown ▮ as he ▮

wears ▮ his head ▮
he shall deceive ▮ himself.

angry ▮
scorned ▮

angry ▮
scorned ▮

If a man publicly denounces ▮
urine.

he shall have lots of power.

49

Blackout 12 "The New Poetry Handbook"
by Mark Strand from Collected Poems (Knopf, 1990), *John Gosslee*

Blade in Hand

Maine took root from woods, farms, sea.
Most of its dining tables
tuck in along the shore
on curved roads
narrow as a sinew,
as a blade.
Coast
like a serrated edge.

From Commerce Street's white tablecloths,
you can stroll at ease
to   a trawler's gutting station
farmer's market
slaughterhouse — though the tongue
prefers an "abbatoir."

Depending on who's hiring,
a high school arm
can grow a rhythm
out of cleave and slit.

French phrases direct menu pairings. Both elide like
tidal seas from Mendelssohn.
Waves draw back and surge, a swallowing motion.
A diner's murmur of "Sublime."

Almost hard by, rubber boots skid in offal.
Thin-honed blades dance
in strokes.

An edged array reduces
every cod caught in St. Vitus dance,
each lowing calf,
to bite-sized —

— fulfilled by sips of wine.

callops butter peas

           Pork chops butter kale

   Cod buerre blanc red peppers   Damariscotta
Saco
       Raw oysters mignonette champagne   Rockland
           Fairfield
ubec
                 Lobster butter "butter and cream"
alibut lemon lettuce under radishes
                    York Hill
        Goat cheese greens vinaigrette

  Yarmouth
    Lamb chops sel-du-mer Red Pontiacs butter green beans

o linger   in the wake of any taste,
iners can be seen to lay aside their knives
nd forks   to consider the four walls,
  or their companions.

nything as fresh as Maine,
  anything a blade is able to divine,
     should be permitted
          dissolution in the recess of the tongue.

Eric Forsbergh

Sentences from the Dim

The abandoned bicycle at the forest's edge,
where factory smoke emerged like a virus
and stalked the air, is what's left
after the mad moon passes,

though the sparrow in its rough round room
in the wreath against my red front door
feels it open and close and dozes.

But I'm sad, because the grocery clerk
in a blue-collared shirt
is more than the stock-boy act

living a bad short story
about stocking frozen peas
over and over without an edit.

John Gosslee

Villanelle of the Ancient Rhymer

They say the rhymer ages with the rhyme:
I used to make my stanzas roar and rage—
now I set my verse to a kinder, gentler time.

It used to be my object all sublime
to strut and fret my lines upon the page:
they say the rhymer ages with the rhyme.

I'd dip my pen in crimson like a crime,
but with the years my soul has grown more sage;
now I set my verse to a kinder, gentler time.

For I had savage mountaintops to climb
and wild and monstrous muses to assuage;
they say the rhymer ages with the rhyme.

Back then I rolled my words in grit and grime,
with joy let loose the beast from out the cage;
now I set my verse to a kinder, gentler time.

I find that now that I am past my prime
I did go gentle into that good age!
they say the rhymer ages with the rhyme:
I set my verse to a kinder, gentler time.

Martha L. Alexander

"V"

*Requiem on the Death of
Winston Churchill, Jan. 25, 1965*

In Blenheim Palace, Woodstock, Oxfordshire
the British Bulldog made his first abode:
at Harrow and at Sandhurst learned the code.
as journalist and soldier to inspire—
to win however long and hard the road,
to fight with all the strength that God can give
and to be born for such a time as this:
to keep the Sceptred Isle from the abyss,
to fight them on the beaches and the field
and on the landing grounds and in the street:
and to surrender never, never yield
the shining shores of England to defeat.
So at his death we celebrate his birth:
in those days there were giants in the earth.

Martha L. Alexander

The Boating Party

an Ekphrastic Poem

Ahhhh sweet Renoir!
The intense talent that drives your hand,
agile, steady and sure of purpose.
Each fleck of paint
building on reality.
Slightest perceptions of light
brings sweating grapes,
shimmering crystal
to life.

I can hear the chatter
of contemplative reverie
voices debating
politics and social issues,
vogue fashion
of the day.
Methodical lapping of water,
saltiness perfuming air,
against rocking boat;
accompaniment to intimate conversation.
I hear
tinkling laughter and giggles from women
amused by male flirtations and flattery.

Your strokes convey the mellowness
brought by flowing crimson wine
taking all my cares away
as I drown in your canvas.
A river of contentedness
making speaking gentlemen
more interesting,
sharpening my ears
to what he has to say.

I taste the warm buttery piquant cheese
as it coats my palate
tart sweet ripeness of grapes.
Wine and companionship
makes the pinching of my corset,
the heat of layered clothing

sweat trickling down my spine,
bearable.
I can feel the texture
of clothes,
persimmon and sunflower yellow
draped on bodies,
Starched lace prickles my neck.
Brightly colored hats worn on heads
adorned with ribbon and silk flowers.

I am in the presence of great talent,
artists and writers,
extreme thinkers of our day.
How deft your hand,
how true your sight,
Oh Renoir…
To make this scene
Come to life!

Sharon Mirtaheri

*Note: An ekphrastic poem is a poem
written about a specific piece of artwork.*

Nobody Flinched

I went back, I had
just passed a bird
in the middle of the road.
It couldn't lift off, its
body was intact, maybe
its legs were gone.
By the time I parked
I could see the wind of
a wheel move it a bit.,
car after car, after car,
a pick-up truck, nobody
flinched, the tonnage
was brutal, left no defining
part on the street. I
wondered about the
nestlings, somewhere
in a tree. Maybe they
weren't that far along
yet, just eggs, bright
robin blue, the starlings
would get those.

Gary Hanna

Song of Gratitude, Sharon Mirtaher

Stopover

The worst
must be over
the geese
are sailing out
on the water,
lining up
to leave
the safe harbor
of Bunting's dock.
They undulate
on waves
falling in together
making ready
in the face
of the raging
wind and sleet,
carefully picking
their way
through ice
to open sea.
All of them
now a mass
of floating feathers
honking
garbled directions
heading straight
into the teeth
of the gale.
Bet they know something
I don't know.

Gary Hanna

Two Birds

For Mark Strand

Across our northern skies, two birds
charge and wheel, the smaller sleek
in hot pursuit. Perhaps the larger

skulked to raid the newborn nest.
Perhaps a tuft of food its beaked
desire lured. Whatever the cause

of this flight's rage, they grapple, peck,
fall and swoop. The chaser nips
the other's tail, ignores the odds,

defying physics, brave in sheer
revenge, aloft. I watch them wing
throughout the morn, then turn to walk

long-rutted fields. Briars, hawthorne
rise to snag. Their gnarled beauty
hosts a single feather, black.

Pia Taavila-Borsheim

Why did the Pigeon Cross the Road?

she was exhausted from
hearing her mate's relentless
squawking over his sorry,
stale life and straggled
out the door to keep
from killing him

she was escaping the snowy egret
who screeched: *Pigeons
are too ugly to live in Florida.
Fly back north, slurp up the
stagnant pools in the city's
potholes if you need water*

she was bored watching PBS
specials on 'the Wonder of Birds,'
re-runs of *Law and Order*,
and she heard the voice of an Elvis
impersonator singing, *Love Me Tender*
from a bar across the street

she ached to feel the soft feathers
of baby birds again, feed chicks
from her own mouth, still
hoping the robin family
near the pond would adopt
her as their Nana—

or, maybe she was just following the chicken.

Beth SKMorris

Rosicrucian tapes

At night and in the morning here, I
hack into the past, to unravel tapes to feel
what hurt I caused,
review as the Rosicrucian would
what others leave for dying.
Tracks of what might have been
disrupt my walk enough to animate
another world. I tire of the role play
and question what possesses me?
When I lie on the new green field
down by the river;
I beg the vultures come
peck at these corpses in my heart
I have not suffered enough to bury.

Mary North

The Family Genome, *Mary Boxley Bullington*

Ocean Fury, *John Truselo*

Love Conquers All

asleep, my whole
body smiles broadly
unconscious
but aware he rests near
an   unspoken comfort
with a partner
who shares
my extant fingerprint

in the night and day
as one, we face   life's time limits
my foggy vision
guided by his   headlight sight
his fumbling feet
supported by my   steady pace
his dulled hearing
filled in by   my good ear

yet ageless hearts thrive
in common ground
we dance   to music
most   don't remember
walk on   familiar clay
from childhood homes
laugh at the   same time
without words exchanged

our love   cannot   be stolen
by mere facts
fading   memory
rusting   judgment
interracial   bias
greedy   heirs
    our full hearts cannot be emptied
    by   events of the day.

Patsy Asuncion

Inspired by *Marriage of Newlyweds,
Ages 96 and 95, Questioned*, ABC News,
Alexandria, VA, September 9, 2014

Earl

The temperature of the rain falls
as the heart does, without warning.
The thicket of thought is dark already,
my clumps of memory yawn
to admit you after this long year
of oblivion. All those wretched nights
spent soused in self-medication collapse
as your voice comes through the open window
as if from another life. The bass, Germanic growl,
the oily vowels working into my brain
like a busy worm, rotting the core
into a fragile pulp that is so much more capable
of love.

My Erl King, luring young girls to your bed
where love is made and unmade again,
the hearth not warm enough to keep
our bodies from cooling after you skin us
down to our lusty, rust-red sinews.

I am on that dark path again, I follow
the fox and the hare to your low doorway,
your body bristling and fresh against the rotting
timber frame. Beyond the door is the smoldering hearth
where I will lay on a bear skin and be lovingly stripped
beneath the hanging bundles of herbs
and strung-up doves.

How glad I was to stop seeing you
in the trees. I can't go back to the horror
of the whole forest staring.

Amanda Williams

Ed

For him, life returned with the bluebirds,
Until this year.

A black nest
In his bluebird house,
With five drained eggs

The bluebirds brought the message about his e
He knew. He told me.

Al Hagy

†The Erl King (Erlkönig) refers to a malevolent forest sprite from Bavarian folklore, the *King of the Elves,* who was known to lurk among the trees and drag unsuspecting travelers to their deaths.

Her Name Was Pelotit

An old man scavenged for roaches.
The last time he took an apple,
they beat him with locust sticks,

thorns gouged his flesh. Left him
to die, face pressed to dirt. Feet
calloused, pumiced by hard rocks.

He hobbled to the spring.
His limp hands held a piece of broken pottery
just hollow enough to scoop up a few sips.

A young woman by the stream slipped
him a clay bowl for water, and a torn piece
of breadcake stuffed just below the rim.

Her clear brown eyes begged for him
to conceal it. Every morning
she'd hide

a loaf of bread inside her pitcher,
stashed it in crevices along the riverbank.
He watched her; found his meal.

He shared it with a lonely cat.
It pounced on the crumbs
that moused to the ground.

He'd fall asleep in the hot alley shade,
away from all the dead bodies carcassing
the streets: the old, the sick, the poor.

One day, guards nudged the old man
slumped against the wall, on cobblestone,
snoring through his beard.

They wondered why he wasn't dead.
So they spied on him shuffling to the stream.
Uncovered his secret.

They quickly lanced the old fool
through the heart—stripped him naked.
Left him to the wolves.

The young woman, they condemned.
And the crowd jeered.
They burned her at the stake.

Her name was Pelotit.

The sky angered. The ground rumbled
then heaved, coughing fire and smoke.
Rocks rained from heaven, fireballs

exploded a hot stench of sulfur
over all the towns in the plain of Jordan.
Lot's heart tremored as he fled.

His wife looked back, for a moment
wondered about her daughter, Pelotit,
but her heart had already hardened
to salt.

John C. Mannone

Based on a rabbinical tradition, *Rabbi Yehudah on Pirqei deR. Eliezer 25*, that
presupposes Lot's third daughter was married to a town official of Sodom

Buwalda

seethe! after you with the push?
from digital nerves an auto-dementia bore
what albatross-shaped symmetries fail to crush
only inner kingdoms (re)store

surge, surge! every shot into the brown
sprung industrious tyrannies, baby gap and pink slime
an insurgent mayberry strikes, storms! loses ground
when pre-cum is shunned on most assembly lines

blinker, bastard! and bellows to mend
a bunk dust on the cuff o' the bum on the plush
'tis enough to bury talibans of shrapnel, friend
or else extinguish whatever is left of the bush

lo! lumpen-handmaidens, sow your own dirges!
suck on them, and spit them, as due recompense
everywhere your gulag graffiti of camouflages
defaces the ancient, boney font of beauty and commonsense

crush! these regimes of anonymous fetish!
     these cults of least resistance!
     holy, holy.
     our heretic heritage, finally,
             hemorrhaging.
straighten bowed back, Buwalda
and drink
how we've all longed for the purer milk of the sword

to sink into the sprawling flesh we need not one tooth but many
to speak to power, not one truth but any

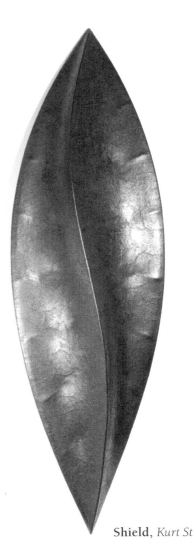

Shield, *Kurt St*

Keith Johnson

Axis Mundi, *Kurt Steger*

Demon Rattle, *Kurt Steger*

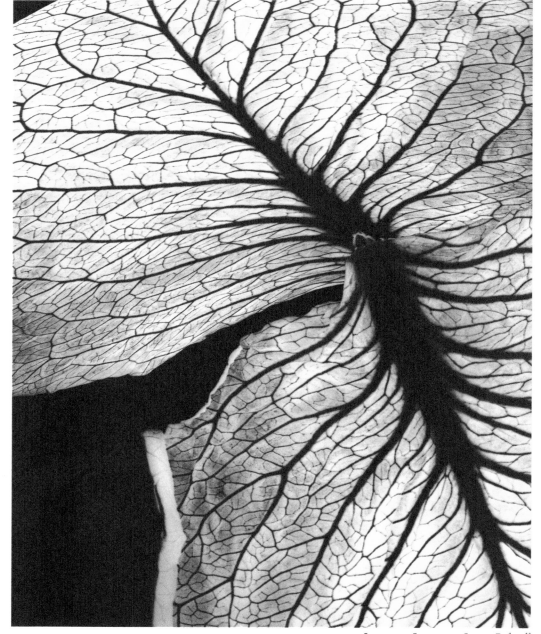

Lettuce, Lettuce, *Susan Bidwell*

The Honorable Gardner P. Hapgood

Hapgood picked up a trowel and stuck it into the compost heap out beside the back door of the kitchen. He turned up a few night crawlers that he dropped into his bait can and headed for the lake. He had already taken his fishing rod, tackle box, thermos jug and a bottle of bourbon down to the shore. His old wooden rowboat was lying a few feet from the water bottom side up. Half the time when he turned the boat over there would be a snake, a fat moccasin, lying underneath it. On this morning there were three of them curled up under the boat. He rolled the boat right side up and chased the snakes away with the oars lying beside the boat, then put the oars over into the boat. He put his tackle box, fishing rod, can of worms, thermos jug and his bottle of bourbon into the boat and pushed it out into the water.

Gardner Hapgood was a big man—tall and weighing over two hundred pounds. When he stepped into the rowboat he almost capsized it. It had been a while since he'd gone out in the boat and his balance wasn't as good as it used to be. He had thought to put on his rubber soled garden boots for good traction and because he knew the boat always leaked a little water after sitting so long in the sun. Once in the water the wood would swell up and seal the leaks. He had meant to bring a life preserver or cushion to sit on but couldn't find one in the garage.

After a few moments rocking back and forth, he steadied the rowboat then pulled on the oars and watched the shoreline of the lake recede until the land was lost in the mist that lay over the surface of the water. The sun coming up over the hills would soon change the mist from grey to pink. Later the sun would burn the mist away and leave a brilliant blue sky.

Out in the middle of the lake, Hapgood shipped his oars and sat very still admiring the flat perfect smoothness of the water. He liked the stillness of the lake in the morning mist and the air so moist you could almost sip it. There had been a heavy rain the day before and the muddy runoff from the hills surrounding the lake had bled into the green water like some kind of murky evil. But it would settle out, drift to the bottom. Still, he had wondered about all the chemical fertilizers and pesticides and herbicides used in agriculture these days and how much eventually made its way into surface water or ground water. Who knows? His wife had taken up organic gardening years ago and brought Hapgood into that shared community of planetary responsibility. But it was a big lake more than thirty acres— bordering other farms and he guessed most of his neighbors on the lake relied on chemicals fixes. Hapgood shook the thought out of his head since there was nothing he could do about it.

On a hot summer day, and he could tell already this was going to be a scorcher, he knew the fish would be near the bottom. He glanced down at the fishing rod at his feet but left it there. Fishing could come later. Or maybe not at all. He was enjoying the silence interrupted only at intervals by a redwing blackbird that acted like he owned all the cattails along the shoreline.

Hapgood didn't want to think about the election he'd lost last November. Most of the time since he left office, he'd kept himself busy re-adjusting to life back on the farm he and his wife, Ellen, owned—an inheritance from her parents. His twelve years in the House of Representatives had given him enough material for a book, and he'd thought about making notes on how best to organize a story that would be fresh with a positive tone to it. Maybe that was the problem.

Since moving back to the farm, Hapgood had stopped watching the news on TV. He let his subscription to the Charlotte Observer expire and couldn't bring himself to renew it. And he'd never gotten the hang of getting news from the Internet. To him, paper in his hands made words more credible than when displayed on a computer screen. Consequently, he hadn't known that his opponent, Holmes Klinger, the man who had taken his seat in Congress, had been indicted until a reporter had called last night for Hapgood's reaction to the story. He should have told the reporter—"No comment." Instead, he had said, "Damn shame." When the reporter asked him to elaborate on that remark, Hapgood told him he would make a formal statement after he had looked over all the charges and Klinger's response.

Hapgood reached down for his thermos jug. He poured himself some black coffee. From the pint bottle of bourbon, he topped up the screw-on coffee cup just as though he was adding cream. He tasted the coffee, then added another hit of the bourbon. It was a good way to start the day, caffeine to sharpen the mind and alcohol to tame it. It was his personal prescription and it had served him well. Not many people knew he took a drink first thing in the morning and it was none of their business anyhow.

Now that the reporter had brought up the troubles of his opponent, the election results wanted to replay in his mind like a lit up billboard. It had been close. Hapgood had lost by two percentage points. He'd been warned about this young upstart, Holmes Klinger. But Hapgood had been popular in his district. While other members of Congress had gotten pitiful job approval ratings—down into the teens even—Hapgood had been an exception. His constituency supported him even when he had taken controversial positions such as supporting a woman's right to make her own reproductive decisions. Being a strong supporter of the right to gun ownership offset the attacks by his critics on the far right who had denounced him for not supporting the rights of the unborn. He'd let it be known he believed in souls, but when a soul enters this realm of our reality it is a religious belief, and our forefathers had established this country on the principle of religious freedom. He emphasized the words freedom and belief. "Belief is a wonderful thing," he would say. "We all own our own belief and it just might be the only thing we really own in this world, and God would not want us to take away another man's belief. In fact, God wants us to honor and respect everyone's belief." It was an answer that seemed to satisfy most of his constituency even if they didn't really understand all that he said.

Hapgood sipped his hard coffee and thought about the warnings from his administrative staff. They went to all those damn Washington parties where everything got discussed and pretty much settled. The petroleum industry wanted hydraulic fracturing and they wanted liability protection. But there was no way in hell he'd ever vote to let any business avoid responsibility for its own actions. He had voted against letting the pharmaceutical industry off the hook when they wanted protection from vaccination lawsuits, and that had cost him support from his colleagues on the banking regulation bill he was supporting.

Hapgood's staff took the daily temperature of issues, and fracking didn't sound many notes with most city dwellers since they didn't give much thought to the source of their tap water. Certainly not the way people who depended on well water did. Hapgood recalled one of his colleagues saying he'd worry about frackin' when the price of a barrel of water equaled the price of a barrel of oil.

Hapgood reached into the can of worms and put a night crawler on his hook and tossed his line out away from the edge of the boat. He could barely make out the hook and sinker descending into the dimly lit murky water. He had allowed about two feet of line between the hook and the red and white cork bobber that floated on the surface like some out of place toy. Now he'd just sit back and watch the bobber and drink his coffee.

After losing his seat in Congress, he could have joined his family in the pickle business. Hapgood Pickles was huge now and that name recognition had helped him get elected in the first place. But he had never wanted to take up the family business. When he was still in high school he decided on a different career. He went to N.C. State and got a degree in history. "Why on earth did anyone need a degree in history," his father. Tazewell Hapgood, had asked him. "There's nothing you can do about what's already been done."

He tried to tell his father that reading history had changed him in ways it was hard to explain. It made him realize how just a few people complicated life for so many others.

"I spent good money getting you an education and you come away from school never having studied the first damn thing about business," Tazewell senior had said.

After college there wasn't much he could do with his degree but teach history at the high school level. And that he did. And he loved doing it and the students thought the world of him. But teaching held his interest for only a few years. After he married, he felt a restless need for a better income. He had met Ellen Davenport at Daniel Morgan High School where he taught. She taught Latin, and in the eyes of the Hapgood family, the two of them became the most useless pair ever to walk down the isle of Wesley Chapel Church.

Hapgood's older brother, Taz, Jr., and his sister, Bertha, had taken over the pickle business and his parents had headed further south and moved into a condo in Vero Beach, Florida

After teaching, Hapgood had taken a job with the Culmann furniture company just down the road from Hickory. He sold wholesale to retail furniture stores all over the East coast. He was so good at what he did, the joke went around that Hapgood could sell trash cans to rednecks.

It was selling furniture that put him on the track to his political career. He was a natural glad-hander and he came across as the most sensible man anyone had ever met. He had a lock on affability and teaching had sharpened his public speaking skills. Then too, he knew how to fill his speeches with just the right slice of history to get his point across. The family name recognition — Hapgood Pickles and the fact that some folks thought the Hapgood family had invented sweet gherkins — did the rest.

When Elton Fordwell retired from Congress, Hapgood's friends urged him to run in the Democratic primary. He did and he trounced his Democratic opponents — all three of them. Then he won the general election in a cakewalk.

Hapgood watched the bobber begin to move around in the water. He knew it was just blue gills pecking at the night crawler on the hook. When a bass would hit the bait, the bobber would plunge all the way under and the line would run out so fast the reel would sing.

He figured they'd run Klinger against him because Klinger was as fresh and wholesome looking as a male college cheerleader (which he had been) and he had a photogenic wife and two young kids. He went to church and acted like he belonged there. He had a style that played out on TV like the perfect soap commercial. And he was a worthy opponent. Of all the men who had ever opposed him, Klinger was the first one Hapgood ever respected. But he knew the party bosses fretted about Klinger's independent streak. And he'd been known to shift his position on issues once he had sorted out all the available facts.

The cork bobbed a moment then went under. Hapgood grabbed his casting rod and let the bass run with the bait. Three, four seconds, then he snatched the line and set the hook. Small mouth bass. He knew it as soon as he started reeling the fish in. They put up the best fight of any fresh water fish in the country. The line raced one direction through the water and then another. The fish broke the surface on one side of the boat then flashed up in the air again on the other side. Hapgood held his casting rod down low over the bow of the boat as he played the bass in. Got to be at least a two pounder, he figured. Hell, maybe more. The bass was putting up such a good fight the boat, now filling with water, was about to tilt over. Hapgood wished he'd thought to bring a net to dip up the fish and get it into the boat. He'd hooked bass before that managed to twist and wiggle and spit out the hook just as you lifted them up out of the water.

Hapgood slowly reeled the bass right up to the edge of the boat and slacked up on the line enough for the fish to stop fighting. He'd let the fish quiet down before trying to scoop him out of the water with his hands. No way was he going to haul a bass this size into the boat just by the hook in its lip and he could see that the fish hadn't swallowed the hook like they sometimes do.

The bass striking the bait so soon had caught Hapgood off guard. When the fish struck the hook, Hapgood had set his bourbon coffee down on the floor of the boat and grabbed the fishing rod. His mind had been so far adrift, he hadn't been paying attention to how much water the boats had taken on. The wood wasn't swelling up like it normally did. Or maybe he'd sprung another leak somewhere. By the time he'd reeled the fish up to the boat his feet were in water nearly up to his anklebone and his coffee cup had tilted over and drifted up to the front of the boat.

Hell, it's a wooden boat, he thought. And it's not gonna sink. With all the water the boat had taken on it was riding low and maybe it'd be easier to bring the fish over the edge. And it was. Hapgood held his fishing rod in his left hand as he lifted the fish then he reached his right arm down into the water and scooped the body of the bass over the edge of the boat where it flipped about before swimming under the seat for the water in the boat was by then deep enough for the fish to stay submerged in its element. Hapgood reached down and stroked the fish like it was some pet. Then he managed to get his hand on the fish long enough to wiggle the hook loose. The bass swam to the back of the boat and turned and swam to the front passing Hapgood's plastic coffee mug and thermos bottle. Hapgood caught the pint bottle of bourbon as it floated by him. "Damn good thing I screwed the top back on," he said to no one unless it was the fish. He grabbed the bottle, twisted off the cap and took a couple of swallows, wincing as each gulp scorched his throat. "Better with coffee," he told the fish that had stopped swimming long enough to look up at Hapgood.

So there he sat in a sinking rowboat drinking bourbon and talking to a fish. The sun had broken through the mist and glowed generously upon Gardner Hapgood who was trying to decide how best to get himself out of this pickle (a favorite expression of the members of his former staff). "Next time I go out in a boat I'm bringing a life jacket. If there is a next time." Maybe the boat wouldn't sink all the way under and some fisherman would come by and throw him a towline. On the other hand, he could wait all day for someone to come by. He took another swallow of bourbon and discussed the matter with the bass. "If I could swim as good as you can I know what I'd do. Actually, I'm gonna do it anyhow. No point in having wet clothes drag me down." So Hapgood pulled off his garden boots and socks, pulled his pants down and peeled the wet pants legs off. He hadn't put on any undershorts so there he sat bare-assed in water now up nearly to the boat seat. Finally he pulled his shirt off and tied it flag-like to the oar handle which he wedged under the seat so that it stuck up into the air. "Maybe somebody will see this. Damn boat's a hazard out here." He slid around and dropped his legs over into the water then tilted forward and tumbled all the way in. The water, so warm on the surface, was surprisingly cold six feet five inches down where his feet started kicking. Though he wasn't much of a swimmer, he thought he could breast stroke and dog paddle and backstroke to shore which looked to be about half a football field away. Playing football in high school he had picked up a fumble and rambled fifty yards into the end zone providing his team the go-ahead touchdown, fifty yards that seemed both an eternity and a flash of time.

Water was not his element. Earth was. Maybe he had misjudged the distance to shore for it seemed not to be getting any closer. When he rolled onto his back and looked at his rowboat all that was visible was the rim of the boat and the oar handles with his shirt hanging limply from it. He wondered if the bass was still inside the boat. It was his boat now. Hapgood rolled back onto his stomach and stroked for shore until exhaustion overtook him. He rolled onto his back and tried to float until he got his wind back. Maybe if he hadn't drunk so much bourbon his will to live would have been stronger. His arms and legs felt so heavy he didn't think he could make one more stroke. And so he sank. Instead of descending into the depths of the lake his feet touched mud. "Well I'll be goddamn," he blurted to the world. "This lake has silted up all the way out to here."

He wadded through the water and onto the shore. He stood there naked looking back in the direction of his boat. "I thought wood floated," he said to the lake. Then he took a few steps toward the house and collapsed onto the grass and lay looking like a huge rag doll someone had carelessly tossed into the yard. He closed his eyes and draped one arm over his face and breathed the blessed air.

"Hap, are you okay? What on earth are you doing lying out there without a stitch on?"

"Sunbathing," he replied without raising his head.

"What did you say?'

"Never mind."

"Hap, are you feeling okay? I thought you were going fishing." The voice was coming from the deck of the house.

"I was. I mean I did."

"Where's the rowboat?"

Hapgood raised a weary arm and pointed out towards the middle of the lake. "Out there."

"I don't see it."

"It's hard to see. Maybe it sunk."

"I'm bringing you a towel. Don't move. Just stay right …."

"I'll be here waiting for you," he said.

In a few moments a shadow fell over his eyes and he opened them to see Ellen leaning over him, a beach towel in her hand. "Hap are you okay? Do you want me to call the doctor?"

"I'm fine. I'm just tired."

"And you've been drinking. I can smell it on your breath."

"Ellen, please sit down. I have something to tell you."

"I know you like to sneak a drink or two early in the morning."

It's not that. I figured something out. Something important."

She lay the towel over her husband's private parts.

"Holmes Klinger was set up," Hapgood said.

"Well, of course he was," Ellen replied, re-adjusting the towel to cover his thighs and stomach.

"No, seriously, he was."

"I said I knew that."

"How did you figure that out?"

"I knew from when you debated him, the young man was likely to go off-script. The news reports, which you pay no attention to anymore, said Klinger had changed his mind on global warming. Well, we know how the system works when they want someone out of the way and they obviously wanted him out."

"Women."

"Of course. I can guarantee they tried to introduce him to just the right woman and God knows they have a stable full each with a different trick."

"How do you know all of this?" Hapgood asked, sitting up and looking at his wife.

"What do you think we talked about when I got together with my friends in Georgetown?"

"Klinger is too early in his marriage to fall for that. And too wholesome."

"Oh I don't know about that. I'm sure they also went after his wife, figuring she couldn't resist designer dresses. She's such a pretty thing. As soon as she saw herself in the mirror, she was hooked. Gifts galore and flying the family off to the Bahamas in a private jet. Oh yes, they'd take Klinger and his wife to dinner with a glittering looking crowd that didn't look all the wholesome once grainy black and white photos came out in the newspapers. Somehow choice photos end up in the hands of the press. Our new member of Congress enjoying the spoils of victory. And now that the federal corruption probe is underway Klinger will have to step aside."

"And the governor can appoint whoever he wants."

"You had to sink your boat to figure all this out?"

"The boat sank because it had a leak. Worse than I thought. And my mind was wandering."

"Obviously. Come on—let's go inside."

Hapgood stood up and wrapped the towel all the way around himself. " Eddie Yardly," he said. "That's who the governor is going to appoint. Foxy Eddie is the best damn lobbyist around and he's kept Carolina tobacco safe from regulators and regulations for years. He worked that angle of "no scientific proof tobacco smoke does any harm" better than any lawyer in the country. And Yardly knows how to take orders and play the game without getting caught. Just the man to carry the no scientific proof banner on global warming."

"You need to call Klinger. Offer to testify in his behalf."

"I'd already decided to do that."

"Now there was a young woman who called first thing this morning. From the Washington Post, she said. I told her you were fishing. She said she would call back but you might want to give her a call. But first you need to take a shower and get dressed. I'll put on some bacon and a pot of grits."

Back Road Buffalo, *Sarah Greene*

November Moment

Stand naked at the edge
Even if only for a little while
Find that November moment
With its crow-calling echoes
Across blanched fields
And husk-dry whispers
Through branch and stalk
And shadows grown long and deep
In the waning sun

Stand naked at the edge
And seek out leafless moments
Even in summer fullness
Offering nothing but themselves
Invitation indelible
To stand exactly where you are
Homeless…
Along the silent edges of where you live
At home at last
Where you are least secure

Stand naked at the edge
Then seat yourself at the table laid
And feast upon the harvest found
In this November moment
Even the brown-backed
And weathered acorn
will take firm root

Steven Bucher

Eclipse

I now know why the ancient people ran and hid
when the moon grew black—

Last night, the moon half dark,
his soul eclipsed by blank tomorrows,
your brother killed himself.

As coyotes mourned,
the moon bloomed white again.

So, always, my love,
there is death and blossom,
death and blossom.

Bones flower
beneath the vast eclipse of sky

and melt like moonlight
into the promise
of white lilacs.

Barbara Friedman Stout

Ghost Wind

Bassett Superior Lines—
Where eternity pivoted
On endlessly spinning table legs,
The miles a man can sand

If he put his whole life
Into the friction—is gone now.
Wood gives up a certain scent
When cut across the heart.

The brows of the long dead
Are dusted with sawdust,
Dusted with gold.
The motes floated through the light

Painted-over windows let in.
They danced in the deafening for decades.
No more. Now the grass grows
Where the factory once stood,

Though the ground still hums.
We come now,
On this first exacting day of fall.
The folks come now

To sell things made by hand
Among EZ Ups, inflatable slides
For the children of the children
Of the men who once

Planed the tables, made the chairs,
Where, before, the oaks and hickories,
Chestnuts and wolves
Of a vast Southeastern forest waited.

Suddenly, high up in the heavens,
A vortex of Styrofoam,
Djinn of plates and napkins,
Spins above the faithful crowd.

Happy canopies are tossed aside,
Delicate legs bent, upended.
Then the dust devil, a circle of white
Rising, flies higher than we can see.

Annie Woodford

News article from WDBJ 7 news: *A small dust devil injured six people at the Bassett Heritage Festival in Henry County Saturday....The dust devil lifted several large, tied down tents into the air, then dropped them down onto a crowd of people.*

California Coast, *Ken Stockton*

Artemis Guest Poet and Artist

Beth Macy, *Guest Poet*

Growing up in the blue-collar town of Urbana, Ohio, Beth Macy knew a lot of factory men and women. She watched her mother soldered lights in an airplane plant, taking care of other people's children after hours while the parents worked in the factories. This was a time when a family could live a comfortable life on factory wages and afford to send their children to college with a little financial aid from the Government.

Macy attended Bowling Green University on a Pell Grant and studied journalism, which prepared her for a profession writing about underdogs and outsiders. She built her career at the Roanoke Times writing features, including her first exploration of the Basset family called "Still Making it in America" that chronicled how Bassett had been cast aside by his family and was left with a small factory in Galax, Virginia. Her reporting work has been given many awards, including a Neiman Fellowship for Journalism at Harvard University.

She has also received numerous awards and national praise for her first book *Factory Man*. It expands on her feature article, telling the full story of how Basset battles offshoring and violations of trade agreements by China, while trying to save jobs in his town. Beth describes the lives of ordinary factory workers once the furniture industry became swept up in the global economy. Her research and insights shed light on how American consumers, corporations and politicians migrated away from USA made products.

Beth Macy has since left the Roanoke Times to work on her second book *Truevine*," a story based in a small 1899 sharecropping community in Franklin County, VA. Keep in touch through her website at intrepidpapergirl.com.

Bill White, *Guest Artist*

Bill White grew up in Philadelphia and received his BFA from the Philadelphia College of Art, now University of the Arts, and his MFA from the Tyler School of Art, Temple University. He was a Professor of Painting and Drawing at Indiana University, then at Hollins University for 39 years, and is now Professor Emeritus. Bill received grants from the Cabell, Mellon & Ford Foundations. He has received the Hollins Distinguished Service Award, the Herta Frietag Faculty Award and the Kendig Individual Artist award.

He is a member of the Midwest Paint Group, and has been a guest artist with Zeuxis, Contemporary Still Life Painters. He exhibits at the Market Gallery in Roanoke & the Nelson Gallery in Lexington, VA. He has had residencies at the Cite International des Art, Paris, France and the Vermont Studio Center, Johnson, VT.

His works have been shown in over 30 solo exhibitions and over 100 juried and invitational group exhibitions in America In 2014 he had a 50 year retrospective of his paintings at Rider University. His works are in a wide range of public and private collections including: Atlantic Credit & Finance Inc., Carilion Clinic, the City of Roanoke, the Garth Newel Music Center, the Hotel Roanoke Conference Center, the Henry Hope Art Museum, Indiana University, the State Museum of Pennsylvania, the Virginia Commonwealth University Medical Center, the Virginia State Bar Association, the E. D. Wilson Museum, Hollins University, Rider University and the Taubman Museum of Art.

He lives and works in Troutville, VA with his wife Linda and their 4 cats.

Artemis Contributors

Adams, Chelsea: *Becoming a Tree*
Chelsea lives on five wooded acres in Riner, VA. Her chapbook, *At Last Light*, was published in 2012 by Finishing Line Press. Her poems have appeared in numerous journals including *Albany Review, Rhino and The Southwestern Review.*

Alexander, Martha Lee.: *Villanelle of the Ancient Rhymer, Requiem for Winston Churchill*
M. Lee Alexander teaches creative writing at William and Mary in Williamsburg, VA. She has published two poetry chapbooks, *Observatory* (2007) and *Folly Bridge* (2011), and has a book-length poetry collection under contract. Her work has appeared in numerous anthologies and has won awards, including the Yeovil Literary Prize (2009). Alexander has performed her work, sometimes with instrumental jazz accompaniment, throughout the mid-Atlantic and internationally.

Almeder, Melanie: *Teakettle*
Melanie's first book, *On Dream Street*, was a finalist for the Walt Whitman award and won the Editor's Prize from Tupelo Press (2007). A 2008 recipient of a Virginia Commission for the Arts Grant, her poems have appeared in *Poetry, Five Points, The Georgia Review, The Seneca Review,* and *The Cortland Review.* She has collaborated with artists in Miami, Ireland, Canada and Finland. She teaches creative writing and contemporary literature at Roanoke College, VA.

Araguz, Jose Angel: *The Astrologer's Lament, Litany for Our Lady of Guadalupe*
Jose Angel Araguz has had work in *Barrow Street, Gulf Coast, Slipstream,* and *Right Hand Pointing.* He is presently pursuing a PhD in Creative Writing at the University of Cincinnati.

Asuncion, Patricia: *Love Conquers All*
Public education, Patsy's ticket from poverty, instilled passion for words in all its creative forms. Presently, her poetry collection, *Cut on the Bias*, is published by Laughing Fire Press and she was guest poet at the Bridgewater International Poetry Festival.

Atkinson, Linda: *Untitled*
Linda is a visual artist and native of Roanoke. She lived for 13 years in California, teaching sculpture and women's studies at the University of California, Santa Cruz. She taught studio art for Hollins University, Radford University and Roanoke College, where she was also gallery director and curator of the Olin Hall Galleries for 11 years. Linda teaches art history at Virginia Western Community College, and is an art consultant and appraiser and maintains an art studio and gallery in Fincastle, VA.

Ayyildiz, Judy Light: *A Deep River*
Judy is the author of 11 books, in 5 genres, including her novel *Forty Thorns* and a poetry collection, *Intervals, from Appalachia to Istanbul.* She is a past President and Editor of *Artemis.*

Barnhart, Francis Curtis: *Coming Into Grace, On Having Come Through It*
Frances is a Graduate of Boston University and The New Seminary (inter-faith), NYC. She is a painter, grandmother of ten, and a writer who has been published in journals including *Artemis*, is author of *The New Woman Warrior's Handbook: Not for Women Only* (under Marjorie Curtis) and is completing her memoir, *Woman Rising: The Beauty of Impermanence.*

Artemis Contributors

Bidwell, Susan: *Lettuce, Lettuce*
Before receiving a formal education in photography, Susan was taught black and white photographic processing by fellow members of the *Alice Springs Camera Club* in Australia. Since returning to the United States, her artwork has won numerous awards and is held in public and private collections. She is a member of *The Market Gallery* in Roanoke, VA.

Blanchard, Jane: *Bridge*
Jane Blanchard studied English at Wake Forest before earning a doctorate from Rutgers. She currently lives and writes in Georgia. Her work has recently appeared in *Mezzo Cammin, Mobius,* and *Orbis*.

Borsheim, Pia: *Two Birds*
Pia is published in *The Adirondack Review, Southern Humanities Review, 32 Poems, Tar River Poetry, The Potomac Review, storySouth, The Southern Review, Measure: A Review of Formal Poetry, Barrow Street, The Broadkill Review* and more. Her poems have also appeared in anthologies, and she has published *Moon on the Meadow: Collected Poems 1977-2007, Two Winters* chap book, and *Notes to David*.

Bucher, Steve: *November Moment*
Steven Bucher is a new poet living on a small farm in the Virginia Piedmont. He is an active member of the Poetry Society of Virginia. Steven's poetry has recently been published in *Calliope Magazine, Blue Heron Review*, and will be included in the upcoming anthology, *NoVA Bards*.

Bullington, Mary Boxley:
A Parable for Poppy, The Family Genome
Mary works primarily in mixed media on paper, especially collage. She is a founding member of *The Market Gallery* in downtown Roanoke, VA, and *Open Studios of Roanoke*. Since 2005, she has served as Tour Coordinator of *Open Studios of Roanoke*. She taught English and the Humanities for over 20 years before becoming a full-time visual artist in 1998.

Cates, Gwen: *Golden Kite*
Gwen Cates creates experimental and playful acrylic paintings, often with collage elements. A native Virginian, Gwen moved to the Santa Ynez Valley, California, with her husband, writer and wine maker, Bill. Gwen studied Fine Art at Virginia Commonwealth University and at Hollins University where she graduated with honors.

Cates, William:
The Honorable Gardner P. Hapgood
Bill Cates is the author of four short story collections and a recent novel, The Growing Season. He is also a photographer and winemaker.

Chichester, Lee: *New York City Window*
Lee has enjoyed a long career as a writer in many disciplines. She and her husband live in Meadows of Dan, where she practices her avocations, including photography and falconry.

Close, Laura: *Where Is the Day Lily's Ancestor?*
Laura Close was awarded the MFA degree in Creative Writing from George Mason University. She is the author of the manuscript *Sound and Sense of Leaves* (2010) and *T Party* (2012), published by iUniverse. Her poems have also appeared in *Raga Zine* and *Jerry Jazz Musician*.

Cooper, Lauren: *Triple Goddess*
Hope Whitby is a published poet, a fiction writer, and haiku aficionado. Her short story in Artemis gives insight into the courage it takes to forgive someone deemed unforgiveable.

Cordova, Karen S.: *The Rope of Intention*
Karen is a writer and business woman who lives in Southern California. She has deep roots both in Southern Colorado and Northern New Mexico. Her work has been published in various journals and is proud to have participated in the 2010 Festival de Flor y Canto at USC.

Dameron, Kim: *Alone in the Mist*
Kim was born and raised in the Roanoke Valley. It was during a fishing trip to the Chesapeake Bay in 2009 that Kim discovered her passion for photography.

Dawe, Kathleen: *Tasia's Wolftrot*
After several art schools and obtaining a BFA from VCU, Kathleen went into graphic design. Other than tending her 200 year old farmhouse in Patrick Henry, her favorite activity is making art and living in the middle of nowhere, which is her favorite somewhere.

Edlich, Ted: *Bristow Hardin, Jr. 1920-1975*
For fifty years, Ted has brought his passion and his principals to Community Action. For the past forty years Ted has led Total Action for Progress as its President and CEI. Through his leadership, TAP developed innovative regional and national models including Virginia Community Action Re-Entry System (Virginia Cares), Project Discovery, Child Health Investment Partnership (CHIP) and National Rural Community Assistance Project.

Epstein, Les: *When I Finally Halt*
Les Epstein is an educator, stage director and writer, based in Roanoke, VA. He serves as Chair of the Department of Theater for Community High School, where he teaches and directs. His poems have appeared in such journals as The *Blind Man's Rainbow* and the *Nisqually Delta Review*. He is the author of ten plays and operas that have enjoyed productions across the country, including off-Broadway's Roy Arias Studio in New York.

Fein, Richard: *The Ethics of Fallen Apples*
Richard Fein was a finalist in The 2004 New York Center for Book Arts Chapbook Competition. A Chapbook of his poems was published by Parallel Press, University of Wisconsin, Madison. He has been published in many web and print journals such as *Cordite, Cortland Review, Reed, Southern Review* and many others.

Ferguson, Maurice:
In Memoriam: For Eric Trethewey
Maurice retired after working in the social services profession for 32 years, mostly with addicts and alcoholics. He joined the *Artemis* poetry group in 1978 and from 1979 to 2001, edited *Artemis* along with Robert Bess and Judy Ayyildiz. His poems have been published in numerous journals and quarterlies, including *Artemis, Melic Review, Samsara Quarterly, Inlet, Metamorphosis, Roanoke Review, Piedmont Literary Review and Foreword Magazine*. He is currently a participant in a poetry group that meets twice a month at Hollins University. He has returned as the literary editor for *Artemis* Journal.

Artemis Contributors

Fitch-Johnson, Janet: *Almost Different*
Janet studied Studio Art and Creative Writing at
Hollins University when it was Hollins College. She
lives with her son on Taylor Mountain in Thaxton, VA.

Fleck, Elaine: *The Goat Dream*
Elaine Fleck is a painter, muralist, and mosaic artist.
Her vision of painting merges her love of textiles and
paint through the thoughtful but playful placing of
fabric on canvas combined with rich and colorful oil
paint. She is a graduate of Virginia Commonwealth
University with a BFA in painting and printmaking.

Forsbergh, Eric: *Blade in Hand*
Forsbergh won the Edgar Allen Poe Memorial from
the Poetry Society of Virginia in 2013 and 2014
and the University of Tennessee prize and Hampton
Roads Writers prize, both in poetry. In 2013, he
published his first book of poetry, *Imagine Morning*.
Richard is a Vietnam veteran and practices dentistry
in Reston, VA.

Francis, Eric: *Velocity Girl*
Most people who know of Eric recognize him
as an astrologer and as the editor of Planet Waves
(PlanetWaves.fm). In other incarnations he is an
investigative reporter who specializes in exposing the
corporate crimes of Monsanto, and a photographer
who has created Book of Blue, a photojournalism
diary from which the photo in *Artemis* is selected.
Those interested in that project may write to him
at blue@bookofblue.com.

Giovanni, Nikki: *At Times Like These*
Nikki is a poet, activist, mother and a distinguished
Professor of English at Virginia Tech. She is a seven

time National Association for the Advancement
of Colored People (NAACP) Image award winner
and the first recipient of the Rosa Parks Woman of
Courage Award. Nikki is the author of twenty-eight
books, a Grammy nominee and holds the Langston
Hughes Medal for Outstanding Poetry, among
other honors.

Goette, Ann: *House Sitting*
Ann Goethe's novel *Midnight Lemonade* was a finalist
for the Barnes and Noble "Discovery Prize." She is
a published playwright, her pose, essays and short
stories have appeared in a number of journals and
magazines. She is the founder of the Blacksburg
New School and a member of the ReNew the New.

Goff, Diane: *Produce*
Diane Porter Goff is a writer and photographer
who has lived in the New River Valley for over fifty
years. Her book, *Riding The Elephant: An Alzheimer's
Journey*, was published in 2009. A graduate of
Hollins University, she has had poetry and short
stories published in journals and magazines such
as *The Sun, Tourane*, and *Southern Distinctions*. Her
work has been part of the theatre productions,
Web Six and *Loose Threads*.

Gosslee, John: *Blackout 12 "The New Poetry
Handbook, Sentences from the Dim"*
American Poet, editor of Fjords Review, iconoclast.

Gowdy, Marjie: *Green Shutters*
Marjie Gowdy writes poetry and stories atop a hill at
the eastern foot of the Blue Ridge Mountains. She has
worked as a newspaper assistant editor, marker, grant
writer, and served for 18 years as founding executive
director at the O'Keefe Museum of Art.

Green, Sarah: *Back Road Buffalo*
Sarah has lived in many places in the U.S. and other countries, but has found nowhere more beautiful than in Floyd County, VA. She is a graduate of the Art Institute of Chicago and her work has been exhibited and published widely in Chicago, the Berkshires, Delaware and Floyd. Sarah resides in Willis, Virginia with her toy Australian Shepherd and 2 rescue Kitties.

Hagy, Al: *Ed*
Al is native of Tazewell, Virginia. He studied at Lynchburg College and the Medical College of Virginia. For more than 50 years he has been a "country doctor," and physician educator for Roanoke Memorial Hospital, the Carilion Health System, and the University of Virginia School of Medicine. He practices Geriatric medicine and is a fledgling poet.

Hanna, Gary: *Nobody Flinched, Stopover*
Gary Hanna has received two Fellowships and five Individual Artist Award from the Delaware Division of the Arts and a Residency Fellowship to the Virginia Center for the Creative Arts. In 2013 he published two chapbooks: *The Homestead Poems* and *Sediment and Other Poems.*

Harkrader: *Fashion Landscape*
Harkrader's work was influenced by the Mountain Lake Symposiums and Workshops, and Web Flash Festival & Conference, France. In 2011, he was selected for an artist residency in Opole, Poland and is published in *Studio Visit, Open Press Studio 2008.* The Holtzman Alumni Center Gallery at Virginia Tech hosted his solo exhibition in 2014-15. His work can be found in public and private collections.

Johnson, Esther: *The Empty Chair*
Esther Whitman Johnson is a former high school counselor from Roanoke, VA., who now travels the globe, volunteering on five continents. Nepal in 2015 will mark her thirteenth international build. Her writing has appeared or is forthcoming in *Main St. Rag, Artemis, Colere, Virginia Literary Journal, Dirty Chai,* and *Virginia Writers Anthology.*

Johnson, Keith T.: *Buwalda*
Keith is a New York native who worked as a film-maker, activist and poet. Completing his master's degree from Virginia Tech, he has continued to pursue his passions in the New River Valley. He lives in Blacksburg with his wife Meredith and cat Petticoat.

Jones, Jason: *Bucolic*
Jason Jones lives Roanoke, VA. New poems are forthcoming in *Saw Palm* and The *Cumberland River Review.*

Jonik, Lauren: *Yellow Rose*
Originally from Pennsylvania, but now based in Brooklyn, New York, Lauren Jonik is a freelance writer and photographer. She currently studies writing at The New School in New York City. Her work can be seen at shootlikeagirlphotography.com

Krassin, Sara: *The Night I Met Your Sister / Jaggin on the Fourth of July*
Sara Krassin is a southern Minnesota poet, bibliophile, and music junkie. She is currently working towards an MFA in creative Writing at Hamlin University.

Artemis Contributors

Krisch, Sam: *Old Burmese, 2011,*
At the Gates of the Wooden Monastery
Sam Krisch is a Roanoke-based fine art photographer known for his dramatic landscapes and iPhone photography. His work has been exhibited throughout the United States and he is Adjunct Curator for Photography at the Taubman Museum of Art.

Leggett, Carolyn: *#170 Falling Fog*
Caroline was born in Roanoke, VA, but moved to Phoenix while in grade school. She was recruited into the US Navy while attending college, serving six years in both the Pacific and Atlantic Oceans. Caroline believes it's sometimes necessary to travel the world to appreciate home. She loves capturing the beauty of Appalachia with her camera. Her works are not edited with post-processing software.

Levine, Eleanor: *Why I Can't Marry a*
WASP from Connecticut: A Revelation
Received While Waiting at 125th Street
Eleanor Levine's work has appeared in *Fiction, the Evergreen Review, Midway Journal* and many other notable publications. She received an MFA in Creative Writing at Hollins University, Virginia.

Lepley, Virginia:
Rural village outside Jinan, China
during Spring Festival
Virginia lives in the Blue Ridge Mountains of southwest Virginia with her husband Tom, and has a deep love for photography, fine art and design, travel, and the Chinese medical and martial arts.

Louthian-Stanley, Gina: *Navigating the Stars*
Gina Louthian-Stanley is an artist, writer, and teacher living in the beautiful Blue Ridge Mountains of Virginia. She is known foremost for monotype printmaking and experimental works in mixed media, especially encaustic and cold wax

Machan, Katharyn: *518 Elizabeth Street,*
Adrienne Rich, Aliens, all Those Years Ago
Kathryn Howd Machan is a professor of writing at Ithaca College. Her poems have appeared in numerous magazines, anthologies and textbooks, such as *The Best American Nonrequired Reading*. Kathryn is the former director of the national Feminist Women's Writing Workshops, Inc.

Mannone, John C.: *Her Name Was Pelotit*
John has work appearing in *The Southern Poetry Anthology* and many other books. He is the poetry editor for *Silver Blade and Abyss & Apex* and adjunct professor of chemistry and physics in east Tennessee. His work has been nominated three times for Pushcart.

Manuel, Margaret: *Sea and Sky*
Margaret was born in New Jersey and has lived in Roanoke, VA since the mid 90s. She is a nursing student at Jefferson College of Health Sciences.

McKernan, John:
Missing The TV Killed by a Shotgun
John McKernan is a retired comma herder and rhyme poacher after 41 years of teaching at Marshall University. He lives in West Virginia where he edits *ABZ Press*. He has published poems in *The Atlantic Monthly, The Paris Review, The New Yorker, Virginia Quarterly Review* and many others. His most recent book is a selected poems, *Resurrection of the Dust.*

McKernan, Llewellyn: *Nude With Mirror*
Llewellyn has a master's degree in creative writing from Brown University. You can find her poems in such journals as *Antietam Review, Kenyon Review, Southern Poetry Review, Appalachian Journal*, and others. Her poems have also been published in thirty-one anthologies and five books, the latest being *The Sound of One Tree Falling*.

Miller, Tim: *Mountain Stranger*
Tim is the education and outreach coordinator for Mountain Castles, Soil and Water Conservation District and is an owner of Muddy Squirrel, an outdoor adventure education business. An avid trail runner, mountain biker and hiker, Tim enjoys getting lost (and sometimes found) in the mountains of Botetourt County.

Mirtaheri, Sharon:
The Boating Party, Song of Gratitude
Sharon graduated from Hollins University with a BA majoring in studio art and minoring in creative writing. Her Masters of Liberal Arts degree, also from Hollins, is in studio art with a concentration in encaustic wax.

Mitchell, Felicia: *Karma, Last Walk, Raphine*
Felicia lives in Washington County, VA, where she teaches English at *Emory & Henry College*. Her work has appeared previously in *Artemis* and many other journals and anthologies. Her most recent collection of poems is *Waltzing with the Horses*.

Modisett, Cara Ellen: *Low Tide*
An essayist, pianist and editor, Cara grew up in Virginia's Shenandoah Valley. She is former editor of *Blue Ridge Country* magazine, and reporter, producer and announcer for WVTF. Currently living in Memphis, Tennessee, she is published in *Still: The Journal, Flycatcher, Braided Brook, Pine Mountain Sand* and *Gravel, Artemis, Roanoke Business, The Roanoker* magazine and four books on the Blue Ridge Parkway.

North, Mary Hayne: *Rosicrucian Tapes*
Mary is part of a group of six artists who performed their works "Loose Threads", at Theatre 101. She enjoys writing, qigong, and a small homeopathic consulting practice.

O'Dell, Molly: *Touch-me-nots*
Molly lives, writes and practices medicine as the public health director for the New River Health District for the Virginia Department of Health. Her poems have appeared in *JAMA, AJN, Chest, Whitefish Review, Platte Valley Review, Magnolia* and several other anthologies.

Partie, David J.: *Standing on Charles Darwin*
David was awarded a Chancellor's Teaching Fellowship at the University of California at Los Angeles where he received a M.A. in German and PhD in Comparative Literature. He has been a professor of English and Modern Languages for over thirty years, and is a translator from German into English.

Pauley, Pauline:
Seven Methods of Invocation, Attic Window
Polly's poetry has been published in *The Hollins Critic, Cider Press Review* and *The Alleghany Review*. She lives with her husband and two children in Botetourt County, VA.

Artemis Contributors

Matt, Prater: *A Ghazal for JoAnn Asbury*
Matt is a poet and writer from Saltville, VA.
A graduate of Radford and Appalachian State
Universities, his work has appeared in *Appalachian
Heritage, Floyd County Moonshine, The Hollins
Critic, James Dickey Review, Motif, Now & Then:
The Appalachian Magazine*, and *Still: The Journal*.
He teaches at Emory & Henry College in Emory, VA.

Prentiss, Sean: *Fragile world*
Sean has been awarded an Albert J. Colton
Fellowship and is a co-editor of an anthology on
the craft of creative nonfiction. His essays, poems,
and stories have appeared in *Brevity, Sycamore
Review, Passage North, Ascent, River Styx, Spoon
River, Nimrod* and others.

Redman, Colleen: *Winter Song*
Colleen Redman is a writer and photographer for
The Floyd Press and other regional publications.
Her poetry has been published nationally, regionally
and online, and has most recently appeared in *Floyd
Moonshine.* "On a good day, my pen is like a dousing
stick that finds a well of meaning I can drink from."

Rhame, Ashley: *The Struggle*
Ashley resides in Roanoke, VA. She is author of
Soul Cry; a collection of poetry, featured poet of
Soul Sessions, and inspirational speaker. Ashely also
coaches youth basketball and writes for her church
Drama Ministry.

Rogers, Jeri Nolan: *Artemis in Paris*
Jeri is the founder of *Artemis Journal*. As a social
activist, the Journal was born in 1977 during her
tenure as Director of a Women's Center where she
created the Journal as a means of expression for her
clients. She operates her publishing and fine art
business from her Barn Studio in Floyd, VA.

Saandholland, Susan: *E/motion*
Susan has lived and worked in Virginia for over
four decades and works in digital photography and
videography. Her work ranges from contemporary
realism to dance, and is best known for her photographic and digital renderings of abstract flow. Her
work may be seen at Saandholland.photoshelter.com.

Sam, David Anthony: *Perfumes of Abandonment*
David has written poetry for over 40 years and
has two collections: *Memories in Clay* and *Dreams
of Wolves* (2014). He lives in Virginia with his
wife Linda, and serves as president of Germanna
Community College. He has been published in
*Carbon Culture Review, The Crucible, The Flagler
Review, The Write Place at the Write Time, The
Summerset Review, The Birds We Pile Loosely*, and
Literature Today.

Schwartz, J.R.: *Rewind The Cowboy*
J. R. Schwartz graduated from Bard College with a
BA in Written Arts for fiction. In the last year her
work switched focus from the experimental short
story form to poetry. Her work can be found on her
bandcamp page, jenniver.bandcamp.com..

Scott, Tricia: *Never Giving Up*
Tricia Scott is a mixed-media artist, photographer,
and home schooling mom. She grew up in Franklin
County, Virginia. After living in Atlanta and New
Jersey, she settled in Roanoke, finding home in an
old farmhouse with a sunny yellow art room at the
top of perfectly creaking stairs.

Selznick, Molly Morikawa: *Solitude*
Molly enjoys the diversity of her craft as a freelance
photographer and graphic designer. Molly's personal
work includes fleeting moments of calm from her
most beloved subjects, her two young boys.

Judith, Skillman: *Kafka's Gray*
Judith's poems are from a working collection about Franz Kafka titled *Kafka's Thistlehead*. She hopes to continue exploring his work and life through these pieces, with the goal of shedding some light on the motivation behind his remarkable works.

SKMorris, Beth: *Why did the pigeon cross the road?*
Beth is an award-winning poet whose collection, *Nowhere to be Found* was published in 2014. She is a participant in the Palm Beach Poetry Festival and is a member of the Hudson Valley Writers Center in Sleepy Hollow, NY. Her poems have appeared in *Poetica, Avocet, The PEN, on line in Bridle Path Press, Lingerpost, and SCREW IOWA!* and in *White Oak Press* and *Poets of the Palm Beaches* anthologies.

Soniat, Katharine: *Sky Talk, Still, Passtime*
Katherine's seventh collection, *Bright Stranger*, is forthcoming in spring 2016. *The Swing Girl* (LSU Press) was selected as Best Collection of 2011 by the Poetry Council of North Carolina. She is widely published and her poems have appeared recently in *World Poetry Portfolio #60*. She was on the faculty at Virginia Tech, Hollins University and teaches in the Great Smokies Writing Program at UNC, Ashville.

Sons, Michele: *Daybreak in the Blue Ridge*
Michele is a Roanoke, Virginia based landscape and portrait photographer with a well developed sense of adventure and a great love of nature. She is especially interested in the transformative power that the natural world can have on us all. Her ongoing project *The Feminine Landscape* features women in the landscape as an exploration of her personal experience of place.

Starling, Doreen: *Passage*
Doreen is an award-winning painter and photographer living with her husband in Roanoke, VA. Her work deals with connecting the physical world with the subtler realms of perception and spirit, with the relationship between the ephemeral and eternal. She holds a Master of Arts in Publications Design from the University of Baltimore.

Steerman, Greg: *Ocean Beach*
Greg is a Chinese medicine practitioner and martial art instructor with a life-long passion for painting. He has a family practice with his wife, Hannah, and lives in Tucson, AZ with their three children.

Steger, Kurt: *Shield, Demon Rattle, Axis Mundi*
Kurt works out of his Brooklyn, NY studio. His work has been exhibited widely in California and Virginia, with three California public art commissions including *The Elders*, a traffic circle tribute to native Grass Valley inhabitants. Kurt views his sculptures as collaborations with nature and hopes his work evokes a deep sence of connection to a primal place.

Stockton, Ken: *Take A Hike, California Coast*
Ken is a self-taught artist from an early age, winning his first award in elementary school. After Virginia Western Community College, he continued on to receive a Bachelor of Fine Arts from San Francisco Art Institute, with honors. For the past six decades his paintings are his diary.

Stout, Barbara: *The Other Child, Eclipse*
Before retiring to Virginia, Barbara taught English and creative writing at Kent School, CT where she received an Honorary Teaching Chair in 2005. Her Publications include a collection of haiku, a chapbook and poems published in journals such as *Amelia, Snowy Egret, The Lyric* and *Hellas*.

Artemis Contributors

Sulkin, Robert: *Elegy for My Lal*
University. His work has been exhibited widely nationwide. In 2009, he was the recipient of a Professional Fellowship from the Virginia Museum of Fine Arts. His exhibition, *Fact, Fiction, Life, Death* was seen in 2014 at the Perspective Gallery, Virginia Tech, and he is scheduled for an exhibition at the Arts Club of Washington in March, 2016.

Teter, Vivian: *The Given Only After,*
The Tenth Dress, Postcard
Vivian's chapbook *Translating a Bridge* was published by Toadlily Press in its Quartet Series *Edge by Edge*. Her poetry has also appeared in *Green Mountains Review, Spoon River, The Missouri Review, The Gettysburg Review, The Anglican Theological Review*, and other journals. She has received two Pushcart Prize nominations and several fellowships from the Virginia Center for the Creative Arts. The Poetry Society of Virginia and the MetroRail Public Arts Project selected one of her poems to be included in an installation at a D.C. metro station.

Trethewey, Eric: *Frost on the Fields,*
November Meditation
The late Eric Trethewey (1943-2014) was the author of numerous books of poetry. *Evening Knowledge* received the Virginia Prize for Poetry in 1990. In addition to his poetry, he was the author of a volume of essays, *Marginal Lessons: Essays on Life and Letters*. His screenplay, *The Home Waltz* won the Virginia Governor's Screenplay Competition. Two of his poems from *Songs & Lamentations* are included in this journal. Beginning in 1987, he published in *Artemis* many times. We were fortunate to have such polished work from a fine poet and friend.

Trethewey, Natasha: *Elegy*
["I think by now the river must be thick"]
Natasha was appointed the Poet Laureate of America by President Obama in June, 2012. In 2007, she was awarded the Pulitzer Prize for Poetry for her 2006 collection of poetry *Native Guard*. She is the Robert W. Woodruff Professor of English and Creative Writing at Emory University where she also directs the Creative Writing Program.

Truselo, John: *Ocean Fury*
John's photos reflect his love and respect for the ocean, which is where he spends most of his free time. An avid surfer, his latest photos are taken with a GoPro Hero camera which lends itself to capturing dynamic action and unique perspectives.

Turner, Page: *Tors Distunxit Amicitiamanet*
(Love Survives with Death Divides)
Page's sculptures are sewn and constructed by hand using heirlooms, preserved animal parts, domestic tools, and sacred objects. She was raised in the heart of the Blue Ridge Mountains, VA. Her work, including *A Stitch in Time Saves Nine* and *Mending: New Uses for Old Traditions,* has been exhibited in numerous galleries, shows and exhibits, and featured in several publications.

Wellman, Irene:
The Widow, Advice for the Young Poet
Irene has been influenced by many poets, but her first influence was her father, a poet and social anthropologist. Her first poem was written at age thirteen, and she became hooked when her father read it out loud. She is still trying to reach out and convey the unsayable feeling, image, passing thought.

Wilbur, Frederick: *Meander Scars, Sweep Thirteen, A Simple Asking*
Frederick, an architectural woodcarver, has authored many articles and three books on this subject. He also has been published in *Shenandoah, Green Mountains Review, The South Carolina Review, Cold Mountain Review, Hampden-Sydney Poetry Review, Southern Poetry Review, Sandy River Review, Slant, New Virginia Review* and *Buddhist Poetry Review*. He lives with his wife of forty five years, in the Blue Ridge Mountains.

Williams, Amanda: *Earl, Innamorata*
Amanda is an MFA Creative Writing student at Hollins University and holds B.A. degrees in English Literature and Theatre. Many of her poems deal with the intersection of cultural values that she experienced growing up in a German/American household living abroad. Amanda is an Early Modern scholar, and has studied Renaissance theatrical texts, dramatic history, and performance. She designs costumes for her historical costuming company, The Bodice Babe.

Wiseman, Dave:
The Last Woolworth's Lunch Counter 1987
Cindy Rinne creates art and writes in San Bernardino, CA. She is an Editor of *Tin Cannon* by PoetrIE and a Poetry Editor for the *Sand Canyon Review*, Crafton Hills College; CA. She won an Honorable Mention in The Rattling Wall Poetry Contest. Cindy is a Guest Author for Saint Julian Press and a founding member of PoetrIE, a California inland empire writing collective.

Woodford, Annie: *Culling, Ghost Wind*
Annie is a poet, reader, and teacher, originally from Southside Virginia, where Virginia and North Carolina meet in a red dirt tangle of back roads and fields that still grows a little Bright Leaf tobacco. Her poetry is informed by this geography and music.

Wyman, Rosemary: *Tree of Life*
Rosemary has a passion for relationship, and her classroom has been full of extensive family and community relationships. Her writing, sculpture, painting and collage integrates her life's experiences, and is grounded in her meditation practice.

Youmans, Marly: *The Dawn Horse*
The most recent poetry books by Marly are *Thaliad, The Foliate Head*, and *The Throne of Psyche*. Recent and forthcoming fiction books are *Glimmerglass, A Death at the White Camellia Orphanage (The Ferrol Sams Award, ForeWord Silver Award)* and *Maze of Blood*. She is a former Roanoke resident, a graduate of Hollins, and a former writer-in-residence in the Hollins Children's Literature M.F.A. You may find her at http://www.thepalaceat2.blogspot.com.

CPSIA information can be obtained at www.ICGtesting.com
Printed in the USA
BVOW10*2339140415

396167BV00003B/4/P